MODERN CAPITAL THEORY

MODERN CAPITAL THEORY

DONALD DEWEY

COLUMBIA UNIVERSITY PRESS

New York and London

Preface

This book ventures a restatement of capital theory with the emphasis mainly upon fundamentals. To the best of my knowledge no closely comparable effort has been made since the publication of Irving Fisher's *The Theory of Interest* in 1930. For while a number of important books treating capital theory have appeared in the intervening years, notably the works of Joan Robinson, Maurice Allais, Erik Lindahl, J. R. Hicks, and Friedrich Hayek, their principal concern has been the exploration of new developments in the subject rather than systematic revision and reconstruction.

I do not doubt that the long reign of Irving Fisher should be attributed largely to the brilliance of his work, for there is no finer individual achievement in modern economics than Fisher's exposition of capital theory. But his long reign also has a less reputable foundation. It can be traced in part to a major style change in economic ideas—the preoccupation with the monetary superstructure of capital theory that began in the 1920s, reached staggering proportions in the 1930s and 1940s, and still warps the teaching of economics in many places. In all important respects, modern capital theory is Fisher's capital theory, which is right and proper. Still, the amendments and extensions (and fashion changes) of the last thirty-five years are, I think, important enough in the aggregate to justify an effort at a restatement. In my discouraged moments, I would almost maintain that the confusion injected into capital theory by the preoccupation with money alone makes the effort worthwhile.

In keeping with its object, this book offers no new or startling thesis. It assumes that the ultimate determinants of capital accumulation are the marginal productivity of investment and the taste for investment—a view of the world explicitly formulated by Fisher nearly sixty years ago and the mark of all good work in capital theory ever since. I suspect that the bosom of every author harbors the secret hope that others will find in his work some merit beyond competent exposition, a good bibliography, or the "convenient arrangement of widely scattered materials." But unhappily for the capital theorist who may so hope, the honor roll in capital theory is a large part of the honor roll in the whole of economic theory. If the list of outstanding contributors is, solely in the interest of brevity, limited to American economists, it still includes J. B. Clark, Irving Fisher, and Frank Knight—and Paul Samuelson and Robert Solow in the present generation. Anyone who begins with this inheritance is not likely to exaggerate his own originality. The extent of my hope is that the reader may find some commendable novelty in the treatment of old and difficult problems, e.g., in representation of investment equilibrium in Chapter VI, the discussion of risk in Chapter X, or the treatment of the demand for money in Chapter XI.

In the following pages, almost no effort is made to show the relevance of the analysis employed to issues of current economic policy. This neglect would seem to require a justification. The capital theory expounded is, I believe, realistic in the sense that it rests upon assumptions that are useful. For example, it assumes throughout that arbitrage in the capital market is perfect. To assume that there is no arbitrage in this market would be quite mad. To specify repeatedly and in detail the degree of imperfection assumed would be tedious and prevent a sharp delineation of the results that arbitrage, however sluggish and imperfect, is always tending to bring about in the capital market. In short, this book employs the method of austere, sustained, and, I regret, largely humorless abstraction that has served economics so well in the past. Given the excruciating complexity of so many of the problems encountered in capital theory, I cannot see that any other method will allow us to cut through to first principles and deal with these problems according to their importance. Either we simplify drastically and ruthlessly in capital theory, or we wander forever in the wilderness of capital intensities, periods of production, money illusions, liquidity traps, Wicksell effects, neutral and nonneutral innovations, internal versus external rates of return on investment, etc.

In writing this book I have received in full measure the kindnesses and courtesies from the university community, night watchmen not excepted, that authors grandly take for granted. My heaviest debts are to James Angell, George Borts, Jacob Mincer, and William Vickrey who interrupted busy work schedules to read and criticize an early draft of the manuscript. I would also like to thank Gary Becker, David Fand, Peter Kenen, and Dave O'Neill for their comments on troublesome chapters; Albert Hart for cheerfully bearing with me on the many occasions when our conversation turned to capital theory; Milton Friedman for general stimulation during his year as visiting professor at Columbia; and Charles Shami for his help in preparing the manuscript for the press. The imperfections of a book, however, lie wholly on the head of him who presumes to write it. This is one of the more equitable features of life.

DONALD DEWEY

New York City
March, 1965

Contents

MODERN CAPITAL THEORY

If the ship strikes upon Scylla, it is dashed in pieces against the rocks; if upon Charybdis, it is swallowed outright. This allegory is pregnant with matter; but we shall only observe the force of it lies here, that a mean be observed in every doctrine and science, and in the rules and axioms thereof, between the rocks of distinctions and the whirlpools of universalities; for these two are the bane and shipwreck of fine geniuses and arts.

—*Francis Bacon*

CHAPTER I Scope and Method

The object of this book is to provide economists with a concise and intelligible introduction to modern capital theory. By modern capital theory we shall mean that part of capital theory which is in a direct line of descent from the work of Irving Fisher and which has been nourished by oral tradition at many universities.

Capital Theory Described

Over the years a wide variety of investigations have been described as "capital theory"; indeed, the term has sometimes seemed to be no more than a synonym for "economic theory." In this book, the principal *raison d'être* of capital theory is narrowly construed. It is to explain how two forces, the technical possiblities that permit capital accumulation and the taste for capital accumulation—or as we shall later call it, the taste for investment—interact to determine simultaneously all of the following magnitudes: the marginal productivity of investment, the rates of interest on loan contracts, the rate of capital accumulation, the rate of income growth, the value of capital assets, and the division of income between investment and consumption. This is enough work for one theory.

Capital theory is often made to serve other purposes as well. It is used to show how the rate of capital formation affects the level of employment, the division of income between "capital" and "labor," and the character of inventions. It is used to show how the marginal productivity of investment, the rates of interest on loan contracts, the rate of capital formation, and the value of capital assets are affected by changes in the money supply and the willingness of people to hold money in preference to other assets. Occasionally it is employed to throw light on the problems that face businessmen when they must choose from among investment alternatives in situations that involve risk. With these refinements and applications of capital theory broadly defined we shall not be much concerned. Our principal aim is to set forth the fundamental axioms and theorems of the subject as clearly as possible.

A knowledge of the refinements and applications of modern capital theory is certainly a worthy thing in an economist. But when it does not rest upon a firm grasp of fundamentals, it is the worst sort of pseudo-knowledge. The young economist who aspires to sit in judgment on the policies of the Federal Reserve System should prepare himself by thinking his way through the classic problems in capital theory that have bothered students of the subject since Thomas Aquinas. Otherwise, he may wind up pontificating about the effects of a change in the rate of interest on consumption and investment without any clear notion of what he means by these terms.

Capital Theory as a Difficult Subject

Eminent authors have described capital theory as the most difficult part of economics. This assertion is not easily proved or disproved; and certainly other parts of economics, especially international trade, imperfect competition, welfare economics, and production under conditions of uncertainty, have a respectable claim to this impressive distinction. But capital theory is difficult enough. Moreover, it is difficult in many different ways and in ways that have no counterparts in other branches of economics. Indeed, the reader who has tenaciously made his way through the most influential books and articles on the subject may properly wonder whether, with the magnificent exception of Irving Fisher,[1] one man's capital theory can ever be fully comprehended by anyone else. The complications that bedevil capital theory are partly mathematical, partly terminological, and mainly methodological. Let us consider them in this order.

In the real world, the stock of capital assets consists of an enormous number of individual items that, having alternative uses, supply an even larger number of different services. Of these individual items in the capital stock, some have useful lives of only a few minutes while others are useful forever. Furthermore, in the real world the composition of this capital stock is constantly changing. So, also, is the composition of the services that it provides. Again, while most capital assets are specialized to a few uses in the short run, they are largely unspecialized in the long run. During its useful life a truck can be economically employed only to transport men and things. When fully depreciated, it is scrap metal available for use in the construction of a virtually unlimited range of capital assets.

Actually there is no limit to the mathematical difficulties that can be introduced into a model that incorporates assumptions appropriate to capital formation in the real world. A major problem in capital theory is to so limit the number of axioms that the techniques of arithmetic, algebra, geometry, and calculus employed will yield useful results. And the amount of simplification necessary before a workable model of capital formation can be devised is drastic indeed. For example, virtually all writers who attempt

---

[1] *The Nature of Capital and Income* (New York, 1906); *The Rate of Interest* (New York, 1907); and *The Theory of Interest* (New York, 1930).

the task dispose of the difficulty created by a heterogeneous output of goods and services by assuming that the economy produces one or at most two commodities.[2] The resort to this simplifying assumption can hardly be avoided, otherwise the investigator is saddled with an unmanageable number of production functions and the necessity of continually correcting for changes in the value of the *numéraire* as the capital stock increases. Again, in capital theory the mathematical complications that intrude because different assets have different spans of useful lives is eliminated either by ignoring it or by positing a fixed relationship between the average length of useful life and the marginal productivity of investment (which is often called the rate of interest).

A lighter cross that the reader must bear in capital theory, though it is heavy enough, is an unstandardized and thoroughly confusing terminology. Identical things are called by different names and different things are called by the same name. The number of different definitions of "capital" employed in the writings of economists defy enumeration. Almost all works on capital theory somewhere introduce the term "investment." It is sometimes used as a synonym for capital, sometimes to describe the process by which the capital stock grows, sometimes to describe the increase in the capital stock itself, and sometimes to denote the purchase of securities. In any modern treatment of capital theory, some term is employed to relate the value of the services yielded by a capital asset during its lifetime to its

[2] In an effort to make capital theory more palatable to beginning students, economists sometimes seek to disguise their use of a one or two commodity model. Thus Mrs. Robinson sugar-coats her austere method by positing that "the commodities purchased for consumption do not alter through time (a loaf is always a loaf, or a shirt a shirt) and they are consumed in fixed proportions, so that, in effect, the output of consumption goods consists of units of a rigid composite commodity." *The Accumulation of Capital* (London, 1958), p. 64.

cost of production. This term has turned up as the marginal rate of return over cost, the marginal efficiency of capital, the rate of profit, the marginal efficiency of investment, and the marginal productivity of capital. Sometimes this return on investment is equated, with or without explanation, to *the* rate of interest. At other times, it is distinguished from the rate of interest, being, in equilibrium, greater or less depending upon the particular definition employed.

The unsatisfactory terminology of capital theory is directly related to the development of the subject and is the visible evidence of its diverse origins. Of the important propositions in capital theory, some were forged in the long controversy that was maintained during the Middle Ages over the ethics of moneylending. Others emerged through the efforts of economists to assess the effects of changes in the value of money on "real" economic activity. Others were a by-product of speculations that sought to explain the process of capital formation. In recent years, not a few of these propositions seem to have been the work of economists whose main object has been logical consistency in economic theory rather than the illumination of any puzzling aspect of "reality." The confusion introduced into capital theory by its historical development is apparent if we contemplate the superficially straightforward statement: "A fall in the rate of interest will cause investment to increase."

To an economist whose familiarity with interest rates has been acquired through work in monetary theory, the statement is both intelligible and correct. Indeed, the whole philosophy of central banking assumes that a change in those rates of interest which the central bank can influence will affect investment. A rise in the rate of interest will curtail investment; a fall in the rate of interest will encourage investment.

To an economist whose knowledge of interest rates is confined to the "pure" capital theory of Frank Knight, the statement makes no sense at all.[3] In his world, the rate of interest is merely another name for the marginal productivity of investment, i.e., the addition to income resulting from an incremental unit of investment divided by this incremental unit. And the marginal productivity of investment is a function of the investment opportunities made possible by technology. According to Knight, there is no reason to believe that there are diminishing returns to investment so long as some part of investment is devoted to the creation of new knowledge.[4] In any event, the rate of interest is governed by forces largely beyond the control of central bankers.

If one is a disciple of Irving Fisher, who unlike Knight allowed for the possibility of diminishing returns to investment, the statement is intelligible but unsatisfactory. Given diminishing returns to investment, an increase in the capital stock occurs, *pari passu*, with a fall in the marginal productivity of investment and, hence, with the rate of interest. Therefore, it is inaccurate to speak of the fall in the rate of interest as the "cause" of the rise in investment.

The economist well-read in capital theory will properly decline to offer a judgment on the above statement until he has been supplied with definitions of "interest rate" and "investment" and the circumstances in which the fall in the interest rate allegedly caused an increase in investment. For reasons that we shall develop in chapter 10 this caution does him credit.

[3] See, for example, "Professor Fisher's Interest Theory," *Journal of Political Economy*, XXXIX (1931), 176–212; "The Quantity of Capital and the Rate of Interest," *Journal of Political Economy*, XLIV (1936), 433–63, 612–42; "Diminishing Returns from Investment," *Journal of Political Economy*, LII (1944), 26–47.

[4] "Diminishing Returns from Investment," pp. 41–43.

Of all the difficulties in capital theory, however, those of methodology are the most formidable. All speculation respecting capital accumulation begins with the self-evident truth that capital accumulation is possible. This truth is sometimes expressed by saying that "capital is productive." But it is well to recognize that there exist two closely related but formally distinct meanings of "capital productivity." Capital is productive in the sense that only a part of the services yielded by the stock of capital assets in some time interval must be used to maintain and replace these assets. After these "costs of production" are met there remains a surplus of services that is commonly called "income." Capital is also productive in the sense that the fraction of this surplus of services which is not "consumed" may be used to increase the surplus by building additional capital assets. That is, income may be "invested." Capital is obviously "productive" in both senses of the word. But why?

An economist recently arrived from Mars and still unconfused by wide reading in the earthly literature on the subject might maintain that the reason is obvious: capital is productive because technical progress is a fact of life. Given a steady and unending stream of inventions—the continuous increase in knowledge—any set of existing capital assets can be used to build a better set of capital assets. Yet in the long history of capital theory, this answer seems never to have been explicitly given, though it is implicit in the writings of many economists.[5]

Instead, much ingenuity has been expended to relate the productivity of capital to the inherent fecundity of nature,

[5] See, for example, Joseph Schumpeter's argument that "the static economy knows no productive interest," and that "the interest aspect" of returns spreads from the profits incident to the successful carrying out of new combinations over the whole economic system. *The Theory of Economic Development*, translated from the German by Redvers Opie (Cambridge, 1934), pp. 157–211.

the technical superiority of future over present goods, or the surplus value generated by applying human labor to inanimate materials. When the earth-bound economist is challenged to give an example of capital productivity he generally replies in one of two ways. He cites the natural growth rates of commercially valuable vegetation or animal populations that form a minute fraction of the capital stock. Trees grow and animals multiply. Alternatively, he points out that capital must be productive since most uses of capital give the investor a positive rate of return, and that this result would not be possible unless most capital assets, in the course of wearing out, yielded up a surplus of services over and above those needed to construct the capital assets that replace them.

Neither of these answers is satisfactory. The references to growing organisms are irrelevant and misleading. They are irrelevant because by far the greatest part of the capital stock consists of specialized machines and skills acquired by education; they are misleading because the "natural" increases in vegetable and animal populations presuppose no shortage of the food and living space that are required to support these increases. The insistence that capital must be productive since most investors secure positive rates of return is merely irrelevant. It tells us nothing about why this result is possible.

The truth is that to explain capital productivity one would have to explain the growth of knowledge itself. For capital accumulation in the real world always involves the use of an existing set of machines and men to create a "better," i.e., more efficient set of men and machines. This achievement presupposes in turn that the economy knows how to create the better man or machine before the task is undertaken. It does not fall to the lot of a mere economist to explain where this knowledge comes from in the first place. In capital theory the economist sets for himself the infinitely more modest task of explaining how capital productivity influences the valuation of capital assets in the market or, perhaps, in the calculations of the Central Planning Commission. The "brute fact" of capital productivity is taken as given.

This sensible and inevitable decision, however, has a startling consequence for methodology. It means that, in capital theory, most instruction is by analogy. One posits a substance that grows, labels it "capital," and likens it to all things of the world which have value in use or value in exchange. Our study of capital theory will be greatly clarified if at the outset we recognize that, most of the time, we are proceeding by analogy. This recognition will save us from the pitfall of assuming that our analysis can always be improved by the introduction of more variables, and that complicated models (with their greater opportunities for error) are necessarily more "realistic" than simple models.

Whether it is possible to devise a capital theory that does not involve the use of analogy is an open question. Professor Samuelson believes that the job can be done and capital theory rigorously developed without the use of the "neoclassical fairy tale" which describes the adventures of some abstract capital substance "that transmutes itself from one machine form to another like a restless reincarnating soul."[6] The alternative, according to Samuelson, is to rely upon

[6] P. A. Samuelson and R. M. Solow, "A Complete Capital Model Involving Heterogeneous Capital Goods," *Quarterly Journal of Economics*, LXX (1956), 537.

"a complete analysis of a great variety of heterogeneous physical capital goods and processes through time." [7]

So far as this writer can see, such a proposal would merely multiply the number of analogies implicit in capital theory. Admittedly it is convenient to assume that "capital" is some jelly-like substance that can take any concrete shape or form, but this assumption is not *per se* especially unrealistic. Assembly lines in the course of wearing out *do* transmute themselves into cars and trucks. The fairy tale enters the picture when one posits that, in the absence of consumption, this jelly-like substance "grows."

Any production function which contains such a built-in growth possibility is a biological analogy. And any production function which permits income to be transformed into some type of capital good contains such a built-in growth possibility. To multiply the number of production functions which incorporate the possibility of capital growth is only to increase the number of fairy tales (analogies).

In capital theory it is convenient but not inevitable that we work with models that produce only one or two products. It is inevitable that we devise some way of coping with the fact that something which can be neither measured nor precisely defined—call it "knowledge"—is both an input and an output in the production process. The biological analogy which likens capital to a growing plant is one way of dealing with this fact.[8] In the real world, it is the existence

---

[7] "Parable and Realism in Capital Theory: The Surrogate Production Function," *Review of Economic Studies*, XXIX (1963), 193.

[8] Readers who may feel that reliance on analogies is hopelessly "unscientific" can obtain some reassurance from professional logicians. While these authorities differ in the enthusiasm with which they accept reasoning by analogy, the consensus seems to be that it is admissible. See, for example, Rudolf Carnap, *Logical Foundations of Probability* (Chicago, 1950), p. 569.

By one view, an analogy is valid to the extent that it permits us to infer from observed "properties, relations, and similarities" those additional

of a body of knowledge that makes possible capital accumulation. In the models of most capital theorists, it is the "natural" growth rate of the capital stock, i.e., the rate prevailing when consumption is zero, that makes possible capital accumulation.

The Achievement of Irving Fisher

In this book our point of departure is the great work of Irving Fisher, the last economist who offered a treatment of capital theory that was at once comprehensive, rigorous, and readable. Fisher's most remarkable achievement, *The Rate of Interest*, published in 1907, is the oldest treatise on active service in American economics. It is consulted by all young economists who decline to be satisfied with the assurance that "interest is mainly a monetary phenomenon" or that "interest is nothing but a phenomenon of the mind." [9] It is the volume mainly drawn upon by writers of textbooks who manage to find a place for capital theory in their crowded chapters. In 1930, toward the end of his working life, Fisher published a revision of his 1907 book as *The Theory of Interest*, which incorporated also material from another earlier book, *The Nature of Capital and Income* (1906). Standing alone, the revision could, without exaggeration, be described as "a wonderful performance, the peak achievement, so far as perfection within its own frame is concerned, of the literature of interest." [10] Since, however, Fisher undertook the revision mainly to gain a wider audience for his ideas, it excluded much and added little.

---

properties, relations, and similarities that would otherwise go unnoticed. H. L. Searles, *Logic and Scientific Methods* (2d ed.; New York, 1956), p. 230.

[9] R. F. Harrod, *Towards a Dynamic Economics* (London, 1949), p. 66.

[10] Joseph Schumpeter, "Irving Fisher's Econometrics," *Econometrica*, XVI (1948), 225.

For Fisher on Interest, the economist should go back to the earlier books.[11]

To praise Fisher is not to denigrate the achievements of other authorities. Frank Knight's contributions to capital theory scattered through more than a dozen brilliant, contentious, and rambling articles are well-known. The more systematic, if less striking, work of Friedrich Hayek[12] deserves more attention than it has so far received. It was Hayek's misfortune to study the fundamentals of capital theory in an era when professional interest in the subject was low and to do so without Knight's flair for controversy. Moreover, the last thirty years have seen the beginning of the end of the "great man" age in economics as in other disciplines. Important contributions no longer appear full-blown in definitive treatises. Increasingly they dribble out piecemeal in the journal articles and notes of able journeymen. Nevertheless, as yet, Fisher's work on capital theory stands apart and above that of other authors. The truth is that, with all his foibles and obsessions, he was probably a genius by any test and certainly the most gifted economist that this country has produced.[13] Still, there are good reasons for attempting a reconstruction and modernization of Fisher's capital theory.

First, his work has the defects of its grandeur. According to Fisher, *The Nature of Capital and Income* was designed to "supply a link long missing between the ideas and usages underlying practical business transactions and the theories of abstract economics." [14] It is written on the principle that

[11] Fisher himself was always inclined to treat his early work in capital theory as definitive. See, for example, his last major article, "Income in Theory and Income Taxation in Practice," *Econometrica*, V (1937), 1–55.

[12] Especially, *The Pure Theory of Capital* (London, 1941).

[13] Fisher's remarkable, varied, and, in many ways tragic, career is described in Irving Norton Fisher, *My Father, Irving Fisher* (New York, 1956).

[14] *The Nature of Capital and Income*, p. vii.

"a good definition should always conform to two tests: it must be useful for scientific analysis; and it must harmonize with popular and instinctive usage."[15] Such a definition does not always exist—even in economics. Consequently, there is an absence of sharp focus in *The Nature of Capital and Income* and the same flaw mars *The Rate of Interest*. Both books are really written at two different levels. Some chapters can only interest economists while others are aimed at businessmen and their undergraduate sons. As Fisher develops his arguments, he frequently rephrases his definitions of basic terms, capital, income, and interest, in the hope of satisfying both groups. A good case can be made that Fisher never really contradicts himself. But his constant revision of definitions means that his arguments are easily misinterpreted.

A case in point is the treatment of "income." Fisher has been criticized for failing to perceive clearly and distinctly that, in reckoning the income of a capital asset, one must always deduct a sum equal to the depreciation on the asset incurred to produce the income.[16] And on one occasion he explicitly rejects this concept of income on the ground that it does not accord with popular usage.[17]

According to the standard actuaries' tables, when the rate of interest is 5 percent, an annuity of $1,000 a year payable for twenty years can be purchased for $12,462. When the rate of interest is 5 percent, the sum of $12,462 will purchase a perpetuity of only $623.10. Most economists would say that the true annual "income" of the annuity is its perpetuity equivalent. Yet Fisher insists that the true annual income of $1,000 a year for twenty years is $1,000

---

[15] *Ibid.*, p. 103.
[16] Knight, "Professor Fisher's Interest Theory," p. 178.
[17] *The Nature of Capital and Income*, p. 111.

a year![18] Later the $1,000 a year for twenty years is described as the income *realized* by an investor and the $623.10 a year as the income *earned* by the investor's capital.[19] Still later, the perpetuity equivalent of $1,000 a year for twenty years (when the rate of interest is 5 percent per annum) is termed *standard* income.[20] Hence, critics who assert that Fisher did not grasp that the provision of income supposes the maintenance of the stock of capital assets intact are in error. But it requires a meticulous reading of Fisher to rebut their charge.

A second and more serious shortcoming of Fisher's capital theory is that it shows the mark of the long controversy that was maintained in the nineteenth century over the respective roles of "capital productivity" and "abstinence" in the determination of interest rates. With the wisdom of hindsight, we know that, in a world of perfect certainty and free exchange, the rate of interest is equal to the marginal productivity of investment in capital assets. The willingness of an investor to abstain from the consumption of income in order to build capital assets affects the rate of capital formation. It does not affect the interest rate unless there happens to be diminishing returns to investment.

In Fisher's work, the marginal productivity of investment appears mostly as the rate of interest, but occasionally as the *marginal rate of return over cost* defined as "that rate which, employed in computing the present worth of all the costs and the present worth of all the returns, will make these two equal." [21] Fisher clearly sees that arbitrage will keep these two rates equal. But he does not see that these two rates are only different names for the same thing. Indeed, at one

[18] *Ibid.*, p. 111.
[19] *Ibid.*, p. 234.
[20] *Ibid.*, pp. 236–37.
[21] *The Theory of Interest*, pp. 168–69.

point, he writes that "many of the elements, both of income and outgo, are materially dependent upon the rate of interest" [22] and, by implication, that a change in the rate of interest can "cause" a change in the marginal rate of return over cost.

In any event, the marginal productivity of investment—the most important idea in modern capital theory—does not hold the center of the stage in Fisher's work. Rather, he repeatedly reiterates the ambiguous proposition that the preference for present enjoyable income over future enjoyable income is the "central fact" in capital theory.[23] Capital productivity is allowed to enter the picture only in so far as it influences this preference. An economist cannot learn the fundamentals of capital theory without Fisher's help. But if his object is a mastery of the subject with economy of effort, Fisher alone is not enough.

Aims and Aspirations

In the chapters that follow, we shall seek to improve upon Fisher in the two areas of weakness noted above. A more direct argument of limited appeal will be used. No effort will be made to assimilate the definitions of capital, interest, and income, commonly employed in the business world. We shall not digress to justify, or seek to camouflage, the use of models, though we shall work with models of the simplest sort. The advisability of proceeding by analogy will be accepted with good grace. Squarely at the center of our version of capital theory will be "the marginal productivity of investment in capital assets." We shall take care to define it with precision.

In addition to restating Fisher on fundamentals, we shall

[22] *Ibid.*, p. 171.
[23] *The Rate of Interest*, pp. 88–92; *The Theory of Interest*, p. 65.

examine three problems in capital theory that held little interest for him. The first is the determination of interest rates when every investment decision is associated with risk. During Fisher's lifetime this problem received no explicit formulation, and the analytical techniques that allow its solution have only become widely known in economics in the last twenty-five years. It is a tribute to Fisher's genius that his casual observations on the connection between risk and interest rates anticipate certain results that we shall derive with the aid of these tools.

The second problem largely ignored by Fisher is the set of complications introduced into capital theory when some commodity takes on the functions of money. In his lifetime Fisher wrote about money at great length, but he took care to emphasize that changes in the value of money are economically significant only to the extent that they are unforeseen. For this reason, he could not believe that changes in the supply of, and demand for, money were worth more than a few paragraphs in an exposition of capital theory that took knowledge of production possibilities as given. My own prejudice is that Fisher's neglect of money in his capital theory was fully justified. Unfortunately, in recent years so much investigation in capital theory has been based on the assumption that interest is mainly a "monetary phenomenon"—whatever this may mean—that it seems advisable to examine at some length the complications introduced by money into the subject.[24]

Finally, we shall consider certain complications that appear in capital theory when production is assumed to be

[24] One writer has recently managed to complete a 45-page survey of developments in interest theory since Keynes without finding any non-monetary treatments worth mentioning. G. S. L. Shackle, "Recent Theories Concerning the Nature and Role of Interest," *Economic Journal*, LXVI (1961), 209–54.

carried on not with capital alone but with two or more "factors of production." These matters were ignored by Fisher because he consistently held to the proposition that capital is the only factor of production. We shall presently accept that Fisher's insistence on this proposition has much to recommend it. But since there is also something to be said for the very popular opposing view, we shall examine income distribution and growth in a model that combines capital with at least one other factor of production.

CHAPTER 2

Capital and Income

According to Irving Fisher, the very first efforts of the beginner in capital theory should be to rid his mind of all prepossessions as to the nature of capital and income.[1] This, alas, is not possible. In order to construct the theory we are obliged to state with some precision what we mean by "capital" and "income." Yet given the manifold meanings that can be—and have been—given to these terms, it seems rash to commit ourselves to a set of definitions until we have canvassed at least the more promising of the many possibilities. Since we must begin somewhere, let us start by recognizing the most widely accepted definition of income and consider how well it serves our purposes. It will be recalled that our object is to explain how the technical possibilities of capital accumulation and the taste for capital accumulation interact to determine simultaneously the marginal productivity of investment, the rate of interest on loans contracts, the rate of income growth, the value of capital assets, and the division of income between investment and consumption.

The Statistician's Definition of Income

Most commonly the annual income of an economy is viewed as the sum of consumption expenditures and net investment expenditures made during the year. This is the same thing as saying that annual income is the sum of con-

---

[1] *The Theory of Interest* (New York, 1930), p. 31.

sumption expenditures and investment expenditures minus the depreciation on plant and equipment incurred to produce the annual income.

An estimate of the annual income so defined can be obtained in one of two ways. We may add up the incomes received by owners of productive agents during the year—wages and salaries, net interest on loans and securities, corporate profits, net rental income of persons, and net income of unincorporate enterprises. Alternatively, we may add up the net value of all consumer goods, consumer services, and capital goods produced during the year. If the economy was supplied with complete records on all commercial transactions, these two methods of estimating annual income should yield the same result since they are but two different ways of looking at the same phenomenon. In the business world, every transaction entails the exchange of money for a good or service. National income accounting assumes that every good or service is worth what is paid for it. Therefore, with accurate bookkeeping the sums paid out for goods and services must equal the sums received by the individuals who sold them.[2]

Four properties of income defined in the above manner, which is the way the statisticians define it, are especially relevant to the study of capital theory. First, except in the unusual circumstances of war, revolution, or severe depression, income always increases over any considerable time interval—a quinquennium, a decade, a century. Possibly there are a few primitive societies known to anthropologists

[2] For a detailed description of techniques of national income accounting see C. S. Shoup, *Principles of National Income Analysis* (Cambridge, 1947); Richard Ruggles and N. D. Ruggles, *National Income Accounts and Income Analysis* (2d ed.; New York, 1956); or E. O. Edwards and P. W. Bell, *The Theory and Measurement of Business Income* (Berkeley, 1961).

for which this proposition does not hold. But it is obviously and tritely true for all of the major, and most of the minor, societies of the world.

Second, income increases over time because the economy is able to equip itself with more and/or better workers, machines, and materials. Indeed these are the only two ways in which income can increase that are worth bothering about.

Third, the more and/or better workers, machines, and materials that increase income are created mainly by investment, i.e., by using manpower and materials (including machines) that could have been used to increase consumption during their period of construction. Admittedly factors other than investment can influence the rate of income growth, for example, the vagaries of climate, the discovery of additional natural resources, or biological mutations that raise or lower the intelligence of human beings. But in technically advanced economies, these other factors are unimportant. Certainly in the American economy of the 1960s annual income is no longer perceptibly affected by chance (and therefore costless) discoveries of useful minerals or by what rainfall does to the agricultural or timber harvest. To say the obvious: today the rate at which national income grows in the American economy is overwhelmingly dependent on the fraction of national income invested and the productivity of this investment.

Finally, no men and few machines last forever. Workers and machines that were created by investment must constantly be maintained and ultimately replaced if national income is not to fall. There are perhaps a few investments which produce indestructible capital assets—a railway tunnel, a highway cut blasted through a mountain, or the diversion of a river into a new channel. But examples of

indestructible capital assets do not come easily to mind.
They are economic curiosities, useful, perhaps, for illus-
trating the meaning of "an income in perpetuity," but
having no statistical significance.

These four properties of "income" as defined by statisticians indicate the main advantages and disadvantages of
the concept for our purposes. On the credit side, the statistician's definition conveys that income is a flow of goods and
services during some interval of time: we ordinarily speak
of income per month, per quarter, or per year. It conveys
also the essential properties of "consumption" and "investment." In national income accounting, consumption is divided into goods and services. The latter are "used up" as
they are produced: one cannot build up an inventory of
haircuts or medical advice. Consumer goods do not immediately disappear when produced, but most of them do
not remain unconsumed for very long. Hence, while it is
always necessary to adjust for changes in the inventory of
consumer goods when reckoning national income, the adjustment is usually small. Most consumer goods are used up
during the calendar or fiscal year in which they are produced. In contrast, the economy's additions to its plant and
equipment that constitute net investment have the common
property of durability; they remain available for the production of consumer goods and services into the next accounting period.

If our object is the concise and intelligible exposition of
capital theory, the statistician's definition of national income is not without its uses. Still, for our purpose, it is
defective in several respects. While it is true that most consumer goods do not remain unconsumed for more than one
calendar year after being produced, the exceptions com-
prise the important category of consumer durables—auto-

mobiles, pleasure yachts, air-conditioners, etc. To classify these durables as a part of current income for the year in which they are produced does considerable violence to reality when the services they yield are spread over many years.

Again, an income which an individual receives by selling his labor services to others is counted as part of national income, e.g., the wage of a longshoreman or the salary of a bookkeeper. So, also, is the income which a self-employed worker receives by selling labor services to others. But no value is placed by national income accounting on the do-it-yourself activities of individuals or the services rendered by women in the home.

The standard definition of income makes an allowance for depreciation on plant and equipment used during the accounting period but none for depreciation on the skills of the labor force. Consequently, in national income accounting, the income earned by a capital asset is not really comparable to the income earned by a worker. If one were to count human beings as part of the capital stock (which, of course, is standard accounting practice in a slave society) our figure for national income each year would have to be revised downward. Much of income as reckoned by statisticians would be revealed for what it really is—the outlay necessary to maintain and replace the skills of the labor force. In primitive economies where most people live near the subsistence level, this revision would perforce cause most of "income" to disappear.

Finally, the criteria that statisticians use to distinguish "consumption" from "investment" are not well suited to fastidious theorizing about these phenomena. For whether a particular good is reckoned as a part of consumption or investment is often determined not by the presence or absence of durability but rather by whether it yields a service that is sold in the market. Thus national income accounting treats a delivery truck as a part of the capital stock but a passenger car as a durable consumer good. In fact, the passenger car is as much a part of the economy's productive capacity as the truck.[3]

From the above remarks it follows that the statistician's definition of income does not imply a definition of capital. A study of the national income accounts merely suggests that there is probably a connection between capital and income. Over any extended period, investment, by definition, is the creation of assets that produce income. But a rise in the numbers or skill of the labor force can also bring about a higher income, so that, in national income accounting, a proposition about income need not also be a proposition about capital.

The Economist's Definition of Income

Many economists, following the trail indicated by Irving Fisher and explicitly blazed by Frank Knight, have reacted against the inconsistencies of the statistician's definitions of capital and income by seeking the ultimate in simplicity. This is done by defining a capital asset as anything that yields a flow of services over time, equating the "product" of the capital asset with this flow of services, and defining "income" as this product minus the services that must be used to keep the capital asset in working order and replace it when it wears out.

Given this usage, there can be no such thing as a "consumer good." A ham sandwich becomes a part of the capital

[3] For further objections to the way in which statisticians keep the national income accounts see J. Bonner and D. S. Lees, "Consumption and Investment," *Journal of Political Economy*, LXXI (1963), 64–75.

stock during its short lifetime. Only some fraction of the "services" that pass from the sandwich to the consumer while he eats and digests it constitute income. Given this usage, "capital" is purely and simply a synonym for "productive power." Capital includes everything useful in production—the skills of human beings, their personal integrity in business transactions, cut flowers, land, raw materials, roads, bridges, buildings, machinery, and even the cohesion of the social order. One can easily make light of the purist's definitions of capital and income. They are of little use to statisticians and add to the burden of the student who is also expected to carry the statistician's definitions around in his head.[4] Nevertheless, in capital theory one cannot do without the purist's definitions of capital and income. The subject abounds with too many pitfalls that can only be avoided by clinging tenaciously to the truth that every proposition about income is also a proposition about capital and, conversely, that every proposition about capital is a proposition about income.

Capital as the Only Factor of Production

Let us accept that a capital asset is anything that yields a flow of services over time, and that the income of this capital asset is the surplus of services above those necessary to maintain and replace it. At first sight this commitment might

---

[4] A case in point is the bewilderment of most students when they first meet the much-discussed proposition of Milton Friedman that the fraction of income consumed is independent of the size of income. This is a novel, arresting, and, given our Keynesian upbringing, apparently incorrect assertion until one realizes that Friedman is employing the purist's definition of income. By this usage, the purchase of a vacuum cleaner or television set is not consumption (as it is in the national income accounts) but investment. Only the services of the vacuum cleaner or television set constitute an addition to consumption. See Milton Friedman, *A Theory of the Consumption Function* (Princeton, 1957).

seem to obviate the need for any attention to the problem of classifying "factors of production" that plays such a large part in the history of capital theory. Are we not left with capital as the only factor of production?

Our choice of definitions does compel this conclusion. And, as suggested above, the acceptance of capital as the only factor of production has one inestimable advantage. It preserves us from the complexities and errors of an analysis which divides the factors of production into, say, labor and capital, and then proceeds to speculate about capital formation on the assumption that, whereas labor can be used to increase capital, capital cannot be used to increase labor.

As a description of the real world, this assumption is hopelessly wrong. People make machines; machines make food; and if food does not make people, it at least makes it possible for them to live long enough to make more machines. The postulate of asymmetry—people make machines but not vice versa—is, of course, the foundation of the so-called labor theory of value and the pointless activity of people who take it seriously. (Perhaps the most notable example of this futility is the effort to measure the quantity of capital in terms of "stored-up labor time.")

To say that capital is the only factor of production is to say that the output of all things useful in production can be increased by investment. To say that capital is a homogeneous factor of production is to say that one set of capital assets can be transformed into another set of capital assets without any sacrifice of consumption. Neither of these propositions is an incontestably accurate description of the investment process in the real world. Therefore, the considerations that have inspired so many different classifications of the factors of production deserve something more than cavalier dismissal.[5] Four are especially worth noting.

First, certain types of capital assets cannot be created by making use of the services of other types of capital assets. (At least no one, as yet, has found a way to manufacture petroleum or coal.) The most we can say is that when investment designed to produce new knowledge is possible, the demand for virtually every known product can be reduced by the creation of substitute products.

Second, since capital assets are ordinarily specialized to a few uses, one type of capital asset can be transformed into a different type only at some cost. The long, acrimonious, and confused controversy in capital theory over whether the real world is characterized by "diminishing returns to investment" really centers on the magnitude of this cost. In the case of the typical capital asset that is "used up" over time, it is sometimes argued that this cost is zero in the long run; that, for example, an economy sacrifices nothing by changing from manual to electric typewriters when the old manual machines would, in any event, have to be replaced by new manual machines. But while a typewriter may be used up over time, the metals from which it is made are not. While there may be no long-run cost of converting manual typewriters into electric typewriters, or indeed any sort of metal machinery, there may be an inescapable cost of converting them into wooden furniture. The diminishing

[5] In discussing definitions of capital we should probably take note of the approach which holds that capital is not a factor of production at all but merely a substance created by combining other factors. This was, in fact, Böhm-Bawerk's nominal view of capital though he really treated capital as a separate factor. My own prejudice is that to say that capital is created by other factors is merely an obscure way of saying that capital is the only factor of production, and that everything useful in production is, in the short run, a specialized capital asset. For a conflicting opinion see André Gabor and I. F. Pearce, "The Place of Money Capital in the Theory of Production," *Quarterly Journal of Economics*, LXXII (1958), 537–57.

returns to investment problem is not to be settled so easily. We shall return to it in chapter 7.

Again, our postulate that capital is the only factor of production does not dispose of the real-world complications that intrude because the production of capital assets is not always a matter of rational calculation. One can show without difficulty that the earning power of a human being is created in the same way as the productive power of a machine, that is, by using services that could have been consumed. But since slave-breeding for profit was abolished in Virginia, it is most improbable that the production of children has, anywhere in the world, been closely governed by profit-and-loss considerations.[6] Nor has it ever been conclusively demonstrated that when parents bequeath earning power to their children, they choose between investments in education and property mainly by comparing prospective rates of return. Not that this possibility should be excluded. Over the last thirty years in the United States, the rate of return on investment in higher education appears to have been suspiciously close to the rate of return on other forms of capital.[7] What is incontrovertible is that children and their parents do weigh costs against prospective returns when choosing between different types of educational investment.

Finally, though capital is viewed as the only factor of

[6] The abolitionist's charge that slave-breeding for profit was a major industry in the upper South before the Civil War has been confirmed by bloodless statistical investigation. See A. H. Conrad and J. R. Meyer, "The Economics of Slavery in the Ante Bellum South," *Journal of Political Economy*, LXVI (1958), 95–130.

[7] One authority estimates that from 1938 through 1954 both the rate of return on investment in college education and the rate of return on business investment (before tax) were in the neighborhood of 9 percent per annum. G. S. Becker, "Underinvestment in College Education?" *American Economic Review*, L (1960), 348–49.

production we must resolve for ourselves an issue debated at length by economists long dead but still not settled to everyone's satisfaction. Is there any meaningful distinction between "capital" viewed as a permanent fund of productive power and "the stock of capital goods" or "things useful in production" viewed as specific objects that are created, destroyed by use, and finally scrapped?

Clearly such a distinction can be made. Depreciation on an existing set of specialized capital assets is a cost that must be incurred in the creation of income. The fact of depreciation means that while an economy is highly specialized in the short run, it is much less so in the long run. Given enough time, some significant fraction of specialized assets can be transformed into other specialized assets without any sacrifice of income. Thus "capital" can be regarded as a fund of abstract productive power which endures forever even though individual capital assets wear out and are replaced by different types of capital assets. The existing set of specialized capital assets provides a flow of services that can be used to create a set identical to itself. Alternatively, this flow of services can be used to create a different set of specialized capital assets. "The bodily tissue of capital lives by destruction and replacement; the utility that is the vital essence of it is, in successful industry, perpetual." [8]

Let us accept that capital viewed as abstract productive power is not the same thing as the stock of capital assets. Is the distinction useful in capital theory? According to some authorities, notably J. B. Clark,[9] one should insist upon the distinction, otherwise, one falls easily into the error of sup-

[8] J. B. Clark, "Capital and Its Earnings," *Publications of the American Economic Association*, III (1889), 98.
[9] "Capital and Its Earnings"; *The Distribution of Wealth* (New York, 1899), pp. 118–21, 150–51.

posing that because particular capital assets are used up, i.e., "consumed," it is also in the nature of capital to be used up. According to other authorities, notably Böhm-Bawerk,[10] the distinction is valid but unimportant; the only abstract productive power that the economy commands is that which is embodied in its existing set of capital assets.

The importance of the distinction between capital as a permanent fund and the set of perishable capital assets really depends upon the assumptions one makes about the role of knowledge in production. If knowledge of production possibilities is taken as a constant, the distinction is unimportant. On this premise, the economy either has the optimum combination of specialized capital assets or it does not. (The combination which is optimal may, of course, be changing continuously.) If the optimum combination obtains, capital in the abstract represents the same permanent income flow as does the existing capital stock. If the optimum combination does not obtain, the economy is in disequilibrium and is presumably moving toward the optimum combination as fast as depreciation of plant, equipment, and human beings will allow.

On the more realistic premise that the knowledge of production possibilities is continuously increasing, the distinction between capital and capital assets is important. Given continuous technical change, the services of the existing set of capital assets can always be used to build a set of new, different, and better capital assets. In the long run, this change-over has no cost. The growth of knowledge in the time that has passed since some assets in the set were created has made some of them obsolete. By definition, an obsolete capital asset is one that it would be wasteful to replace when

[10] "Capital and Interest Once More," *Quarterly Journal of Economics,* XXI (1906), 1–21; XXII (1907), 247–82.

fully depreciated. Therefore, so long as one asset in the capital stock is obsolete, the economy's present income is always less than its future income even though no part of present income is invested.

We can make the above point in different words. The value of the existing set of capital assets depends upon what it can produce. *Ceteris paribus*, this value is increased when technical progress makes obsolete one type of capital asset and so causes some assets in the set (including, possibly, men or machines of the obsolete type) to be shifted to the production of assets of the new and better type. Technical progress always confers a bonus, for the amount of services yielded up by the stock of capital assets during its useful life is greater than it would have been had technical progress suddenly ceased when the stock was first placed in service. Technical progress can, of course, reduce or even destroy entirely the value of individual capital assets. But it cannot reduce the value of "capital assets in general" since they are the means to produce the new and better assets.

In short, the distinction between capital viewed as a permanent fund of productive power—"pure" or "true" capital in the language of J. B. Clark—and the specialized assets that form the existing capital stock is mainly useful because it directs attention to an important, if obvious, truth. In the real world, "the maintenance of the capital stock intact" is secured by using an existing set of specialized assets, not to perpetuate themselves *ad infinitum*, but to create a different and better set of specialized assets.

Capital as Discounted Income

One widely used definition of capital we have not considered in this chapter. In the real world, different capital assets produce different types of services. One cannot compare one asset with another without having a *numéraire* in which the different types of services can be expressed, and an interest rate that states the terms upon which present consumption can be converted into future income. Therefore, many writers make "capital" a synonym for "capital value" or "value of the capital stock" and affirm that "the quantity of capital is the economy's income (in perpetuity) divided by the rate of interest." When income is increasing, a further complication intrudes because the purchasing power of the *numéraire* in terms of the services that it buys may also be changing. If so, one cannot measure a change in the quantity of capital (defined as discounted income) without first devising a set of index numbers that will allow the quantity of capital to be expressed in terms of a *numéraire* of constant purchasing power.

The definition that equates capital with "real income" discounted by the rate of interest is not, strictly speaking, wrong. The use of this definition, however, makes impossible a precise formulation of the most important single concept in capital theory—the marginal productivity of investment. This limitation we examine at length in chapter 4.

In empirical work, no estimate of the quantity of capital can be made unless one is given "income" and some rate at which to discount it. In capital theory this restriction need not apply. The economist is at liberty to posit that capital is a homogeneous substance which provides only one type of useful service. When this is done, "the quantity of capital" is a physical magnitude that, at any given moment, "exists." It does not depend upon either the income that it produces or the rate of interest at which this income is discounted.

Recapitulation

Henceforth our concern will mainly be with those forces that produce changes in the stock of capital assets. We define a capital asset as anything that furnishes a service over time. By the "product" of a capital asset we shall mean the flow of services that it yields during some interval of time. By the "income" of a capital asset, we shall mean this product minus the outlay necessary to maintain and replace that portion of the capital asset "used up" in producing this product. We accept that given a continuous growth of knowledge, some assets in the capital stock are always obsolete; so that, given enough time, the economy can always increase its income even though no part of income is invested. This increase is secured by replacing obsolete assets that are fully depreciated with new and better assets. The view that capital is discounted real income is, for the moment, noted but not endorsed.

CHAPTER 3   Capital Productivity

In capital theory two ideas are important above all others. The first has, with fair consistency, been discussed by economists under the title, "capital productivity." The second has been given a multitude of names, though it is most commonly known as "abstinence," "waiting," or "time-preference." We shall presently call it by yet another name, "the taste for investment." Neither of these ideas is new. Still, if we would avoid the unprofitable controversies of the past, we must take care to formulate them with precision.

An Ancient Controversy

The history of economic doctrine abounds with conflicts whose leading issues are scarcely intelligible to modern readers. One of the longest and murkiest was maintained by authors who sought to explain "the nature and necessity of interest." In its early stages the conflict consisted mostly of naive moralizing about the ethics of moneylending. Was a lender ever justified in charging interest to the borrower? If so, under what circumstances and subject to what limitations? In its later stages, the conflict was maintained by writers who traced the existence of interest mainly to the productivity of investment in capital assets in opposition to writers who traced it mainly to the ubiquitous preference for present over future consumption which insures that people will not willingly "abstain" from consumption unless they are rewarded for doing so. Even in its later stages the debate on the *raison d'être* of interest was extremely confused. It did, however, finally establish that capital productivity and the taste for investment are real and distinct phenomena. The great number of books, tracts, and articles on interest that have appeared over the years were not written in vain.

A clear formulation of the ideas of capital productivity and the taste for investment was long impeded by two related difficulties (we generalize with the wisdom of hindsight). The first was the ever-present danger of falling into the trap of circular reasoning. The second was the difficulty of framing a convincing explanation of why the construction of inanimate capital assets should be "productive." Consider the circularity danger.

Many writers have contended that the existence of interest is rooted in the "fact" that any man in full possession of his mental faculties will, at most times and places, prefer to have ten dollars now rather than ten dollars later. This proposition states a self-evident truth. But in a world of interest rates, there is an obvious reason why one's preference is for ten dollars now. By taking the ten dollars now and loaning it out at interest, one can have more than ten dollars later. Again, if ten dollars now can be used to increase one's income by building a capital asset—if capital is productive—the rational man will always elect to have the ten dollars now. In order to discern a man's preference for present as against future income, it is necessary that he choose between ten dollars' worth of services to be consumed now and ten dollars' worth of services to be consumed later, and the choice must be made in a context that allows neither loans at interest nor the construction of capital assets.

The pitfall of circular reasoning in capital theory could have been more easily avoided if those authors who perceived the connection between interest rates and capital productivity had been more adept at explaining it to skeptics. In an uncertain world where "in life we are in the midst of death" skeptics were satisfied that there was a simple and obvious explanation of why interest was paid. Present consumption is certain, future consumption more doubtful. Therefore, nobody willingly gives up ten dollars now unless he is promised more than ten dollars later.

The task of economists who advocated a capital productivity theory of interest was to explain to skeptics that the latter's views on interest were true but irrelevant to the real world. In an economy where capital accumulation was impossible, e.g., in a prison camp, there would be a rate of interest.[1] It would be determined wholly by the inmates' preference for present over future consumption in relation to the expected flow of consumable things—food parcels, cigarettes, etc. But in the real world capital accumulation is possible, hence, the rate of interest depends mainly upon the terms upon which present income can be exchanged for future income by foregoing consumption to create capital assets. Unhappily, when economists who stressed the importance of capital productivity as an explanation of interest sought to explain what they meant by capital productivity, the results were often very curious.

Three Explanations of Capital Productivity

In chapter 1, we noted that the concept of capital productivity is implicit in the "fact" of capital accumulation, and that capital is productive in two distinguishable ways. The

[1] The problem of interest in the case where "all sources of services are permanent and not capable of being reproduced" is considered in Milton Friedman, *Price Theory: A Provisional Text* (Chicago, 1962), pp. 246–48, and P. A. Samuelson, "An Exact Consumption-Loan Model of Interest With or Without the Social Contrivance of Money," *Journal of Political Economy* LXVI (1958), 467–82.

process of production generates a surplus of services over and above those needed to maintain and replace the individual capital assets "used up" in the process. By definition, this surplus is income. The size of this surplus can be increased over time if some fraction is used to construct additional capital assets. The assumption that income can be increased by "investment" or "saving" has been common currency for at least four hundred years. Even so, capital productivity is still one of the haziest ideas in economic theory,[2] and the young Ph.D. candidate can soon be reduced to desperation if pressed for an explanation of why income can be increased by adding to the stock of capital assets. Everyone knows that capital is productive. But why?

Historically, three theories have been advanced to explain why income can be increased by building additional capital assets. In the work of eighteenth-century authors, notably the statesman Turgot,[3] the productivity of capital is traced to the inherent fecundity of nature—vegetation grows and animals multiply.[4] An economy, by refraining from consuming all of its annual harvest of wheat or lambs, can have a larger harvest of wheat or lambs next year. Nature has, in effect, established for agriculture a series of

[2] No originality can be claimed for this complaint. Long ago Böhm-Bawerk began his examination of capital productivity by observing it to be encrusted with "a superabundance of obscurity, error, confusion, and fallacious conclusions of every sort." *Capital and Interest*, translated from the fourth German edition by G. D. Huncke and others (3 vols.; South Holland, Ill., 1959), I, 73.

[3] *Reflexions sur la formation et la distribution des richesses* (Paris, 1766).

[4] Turgot has a good claim to recognition as the first author who clearly perceived the connection between interest and capital productivity. But many writers before him had caught a glimpse of the tie. The doctrine rejected by Thomas Aquinas but accepted by some later Schoolmen that a lender is entitled to charge for *lucrum cessans*—the profits that he could have made had he used the funds loaned out in his own business—really assumes the productivity of capital. For the finer points of medieval interest theory, see J. T. Noonan, Jr., *The Scholastic Analysis of Usury* (Cambridge, 1957).

natural rates of return on investment—a wheat rate, a lamb rate, etc. According to Turgot, no such natural rates pertain to the inanimate machines, materials, and goods that are manufactured and exchanged. Still, investment in manufacturing and commerce must carry a positive rate of return, otherwise merchants would invest in agriculture. The economic productivity of investment outside agriculture (measured in terms of money or a *numéraire*) is derived from the physical productivity of investment within agriculture.

In an economy whose efforts are devoted mainly to near subsistence agriculture, this explanation has a specious plausibility. (Its plausibility is specious because any curtailment of consumption in such an economy is likely to lead to a destruction of human capital through malnutrition and starvation.) In more advanced economies where livestock and growing crops constitute but a small fraction of the stock of capital assets, "naive" explanations of capital productivity are not taken seriously. References to growing trees, ripening wheat, aging wine, and the natural growth rate of rabbit populations have not disappeared from capital theory. Nor are they likely to disappear given the pedagogical returns to be had by resorting to analogy in this branch of economics. These references, however, now serve not to explain the productivity of capital but to illustrate its properties on the assumption that it exists.

While naive explanations of capital productivity long ago lost most of their intellectual respectability, one may claim for them a major virtue lacking in much later work on capital theory. They stressed the important truth that the productivity of capital is a physical fact of life—not a matter of the subjective valuations placed upon present as against future goods. Capital accumulation is possible because commodities can be used to make more commodities. Even Irving Fisher forgot this truth to the point of writing:

The rate of physical productivity is evidently not the rate of interest. The rate of physical productivity is not ordinarily even the same kind of magnitude as the rate of interest. Bushels of wheat produced per acre is an entirely different sort of ratio from the rate per cent of the net value of the yield of land relative to the value of the land. Interest is a rate per cent, an abstract number. Physical productivity is a rate of one concrete thing relatively to another concrete thing incommensurable with the first.[5]

Admittedly, capital productivity is almost always measured with the aid of a money commodity and a price index. Nevertheless, capital productivity is rooted in the fact of physical productivity. Consider Fisher's fruitgrowing example. By his argument:

If an orchard could in some sudden and *wholly unexpected* way be made to yield double its original crop per acre, only its yield in the sense of physical productivity would be doubled; its yield in the sense of the rate of interest would not necessarily be affected at all, certainly not doubled, because the value of the orchard would automatically advance with an increase in its value productivity.[6]

Fisher's argument is correct. But it is correct only because the orchard is so small a fraction of the economy's capital stock that a change in its physical productivity cannot significantly affect the rate of interest. The unimportance of the orchard does not alter the truth that a positive rate of return (in constant dollars) in, say applegrowing, is possible only when one or more of the following conditions are pres-

[5] *The Theory of Interest* (New York, 1930), p. 57.
[6] *Ibid.*, pp. 56–57.

ent: 1) Apples can be used to grow more apples; 2) Apples can be used to increase the output of some other commodity, e.g., as fertilizer in the raising of grass; 3) The physical output of some other commodity offered in exchange for apples can be increased, so that the price of apples rises because they have become more scarce relative to this other commodity.

It may be objected that a fourth possibility should be recognized. Will not a simple increase in the taste for apples during the period of production make for a positive rate of return on investment in applegrowing? This is certainly possible. If, however, the physical output of the commodities offered in exchange for apples has not risen, then an increase in the demand for apples is a fall in the demand for these other commodities. In this circumstance, a positive rate of return in applegrowing is possible only because a lower rate of return (in constant dollars) characterizes other economic activities. Clearly, when a positive rate of return is posited for all investments, a positive rate of return in applegrowing cannot be ascribed solely to an increase in the taste for apples.

Turgot and his followers were wholly correct when they traced the existence of interest to the physical productivity of capital. Their error lay in the assumption that only investment in agriculture is physically productive. But this error should be viewed charitably since, in capital theory, the distinction between those investments which are physically productive and those which are not is perfectly valid. For example, when real income increases more rapidly than the stock of money, the value of money increases and one obtains a positive return by holding money. Yet the productivity of not spending money, measured in terms of what money buys, is obviously derived from the physical productivity of other investments. To say that "capital is productive" is not to say that all goods can be used to make more goods—only that some goods can be used to make more goods. It is doubtful that barber chairs can be used to increase the output of barber chairs or anything else (even haircuts) in any statistically significant way. The physical productivity of machine tools used to make other machine tools is self-evident.

Some nineteenth-century writers sought to establish the productivity of capital without resort to biological causation by using some version of the labor theory of value. In Marx, for example, the possibility of capital accumulation is ascribed to the mysteries of the "labor process." Inanimate capital assets—the means of production—"never transfer more value to the product than they themselves lose during the labour-process by the destruction of their own use-value." [7] It is the application of labor to the means of production that creates the surplus value which can be embodied in an addition to the means of production.

Hence, the labourer preserves the values of the consumed means of production, or transfers them as portions of its value to the product, not by virtue of his additional labour, abstractly considered, but by virtue of the particular useful character of that labour, by virtue of its special productive form. In so far, then, as labour is such specific productive activity, in so far as it is spinning, weaving, or forging, it raises, by mere contact, the means of production from the dead, makes them living factors of the labour-process, and combines with them to form the new products. [8]

[7] *Capital: A Critical Analysis of Capitalist Production*, translated from the third German edition by Samuel Moore and George Aveling (London, 1886), p. 186.
[8] *Ibid.*, p. 182.

The labor theory of value is an intellectual curiosity that economists have long since abandoned to theologians. The principal explanation of capital productivity that they put in its place, however, was no improvement.

Since the work of Böhm-Bawerk, most writers on capital theory have assumed that, at any moment, there exists a spectrum of alternative production techniques, and income can be increased, at a cost, by substituting certain of these techniques for others. By the conventional view, income can be increased by substituting techniques that yield their flow of services over a longer period for those that yield their flow in some shorter interval. "It is a technological fact of life that you can get more future consumption by using indirect or roundabout methods." [9]

We cannot be sure who first used the efforts of Robinson Crusoe to improve his comfort to illustrate this spectrum and the cost of substituting one technique for another. But over the years innumerable students have been introduced to capital theory by being persuaded that Crusoe could increase his catch of fish by eating less for a few days while he devoted his labor to building a boat. In the work of Böhm-Bawerk, the Crusoe example is generalized in the proposition that roundabout methods of production are, in general, more efficient than less roundabout methods. That is, if an economy wishes to increase its income (in perpetuity) it can do so by substituting capital assets that take a longer time to build for those which take a shorter time.[10] From this premise Böhm-Bawerk inferred that,

[9] P. A. Samuelson, *Economics: An Introductory Analysis* (5th ed.; New York, 1961), p. 645.

[10] "It is an elementary fact of human experience that time consuming roundabout methods of production are more productive. That means that, given equal quantities of the means of production, the more time a method of production consumes, the greater will be the output it produces." *Capital and Interest*, II, 273.

should the willingness of investors to abstain from consumption increase, more of the more roundabout methods of production will be introduced and, hence, the (average) period of production will lengthen.[11] Böhm-Bawerk did not feel it necessary to offer an explanation of why the roundabout methods were more productive; such speculation was left to others.[12] For him their superiority in most industries was a fact that can be confirmed by observation.

A minor criticism of Böhm-Bawerk's argument is that it rests on a premise that may not be correct. Whether an increase in the willingness to save would lengthen the period of production of capital assets is a matter for empirical investigation. Some production techniques in the spectrum that could profitably be employed only at a very low rate of interest might require the construction of assets with very short periods of production.

There is, however, a more fundamental objection to the argument. Even if capital accumulation is associated with an increase in the average useful life of capital assets, this

[11] Most economists would now say that "the period of production" extends from the moment that the first expense is incurred in the construction of a capital asset to the moment that it yields its last useful services and is melted down for scrap or, in the case of a human being, retired. In older works on capital theory, some part of this interval, usually the period during which costs are incurred but no services obtained, was often treated as *the* period of production of a capital asset. Böhm-Bawerk does not explicitly define the term. By my reading, he usually uses it to designate this shorter gestation period of the capital asset. See *Capital and Interest*, II, 280–81. For the various meanings that Böhm-Bawerk gave to the period of production, see H. T. N. Gaitskell, "Notes on the Period of Production," *Zeitschrift für Nationalökonomie*, VII (1936), 577–88.

[12] See, for example, *Capital and Its Structure*, pp. 81–83. The gist of Lachmann's thesis seems to be that the roundabout method of production is technically superior to the direct because it permits production with "a higher degree of division of capital," i.e., a more specialized capital structure. Unhappily, Lachmann's cryptic exposition of his thesis does not make clear why this relationship should hold; indeed, the reader is left without a clue as to how one would set about measuring the degree of capital division.

increase has no economic significance. In the construction of a capital asset, the crucial consideration is not time but *cost in relation to income*. The willingness of people to save will produce an increase in the stock of capital assets, assuming always that capital accumulation is possible. As a result, the average period of production of capital assets may increase, decrease, or remain unchanged. This change, however, is an incidental by-product of the change in the stock of capital assets. To the investor, the important datum on a capital asset is neither the time required to construct it nor the length of its useful life. The important datum is its rate of return over cost. The asset's period of production enters the picture only because, in a world where most rates of interest are above zero, time is an element of cost.

Böhm-Bawerk's emphasis on the period of production is properly open to objection on the ground that it uncritically equates time with cost. Yet even this objection does not indicate the major source of confusion in his effort to explain capital productivity. Rather the major obscurities and errors in his capital theory resulted because he sought to analyze capital accumulation within the context of a static state—one where technology is "given." In the real world there clearly exists a spectrum of alternative production techniques all "given," and, clearly, income can be increased, at a cost, by substituting certain techniques for others. However, two features of this real-world spectrum ought to be noted.

First, certain of the alternative production techniques are of recent origin. They are represented by inventions still on the drawing board and inventions whose adoption is being delayed by investment sunk in "inferior" techniques. These inferior techniques are embodied in a set of capital assets which, by definition, are obsolete. And while capital assets of an obsolete type will remain in use until fully depreciated (i.e., until total receipts no longer cover total variable costs), no additional capital assets of this type will be built.

Second, the existence of the recent inventions insures that the economy, over time, can increase its income without cost, i.e., without abstaining from the consumption of some part of income. (We must never, in any circumstance, forget that the production of income presupposes that the economy abstains from consuming any part of its capital stock.) It need only use resources freed by depreciation to replace obsolete men and machines with superior new men and machines.

Capital Accumulation with a "Given" Technology

It is also true that an economy can add to its income at a cost. Indeed, all theorizing about capital accumulation assumes that income can be created by saving, i.e., by not consuming all of current income. But here one must tread carefully. To the extent that an economy saves by constructing capital assets that embody the results of recent research and development, one reason for "capital productivity" is self-evident. The construction of new type capital assets *is* the effective application of new knowledge. In this context, to say that investment in capital assets is productive is only to say that income can be raised by making use of the results of research and development.

Suppose, however, that one inhabits the static state of economists' lore where not a single type of man or machine is obsolete—where the knowledge of production techniques has remained unchanged for as long as anyone can remember. In this situation, is there any reason to suppose that the use of services of capital assets that constitute income to construct additional capital assets will raise income "even-

tually"? Or, to insure this result, must one posit the presence
of continuous innovation? Must one assume that there always exists at least one obsolete type of man or machine in
order to establish the technical possibility of capital accumulation?

Given the predilection of economists for analyzing problems within the context of a static state, it is probably well
that this question should be asked. But I am not sure that
any good end would be served by trying to answer it. For
our purpose it will suffice to affirm an obvious truth: the
only societies which have ever had enough capital accumulation to suggest the need for an explanation of capital
productivity are those characterized by continuous innovation. While an increase in knowledge that produces continuous innovation may not be the only source of income
growth, it is overwhelmingly the most important source.
The effort to establish the possibility of capital accumulation, in an economic model where technology is given, and
the most efficient production techniques have already been
adopted, is best avoided. It can only lead back to Turgot's
natural fecundity of nature, the unfathomable mysteries of
Marx's "labor process," Böhm-Bawerk's superiority of the
more roundabout method of production, or some equally
unconvincing explanation.

In modern capital theory, then, the notion of the static
state occupies a very insecure place. In the real world, the
knowledge of production possibilities is continually being
increased by plodding journeymen efforts in research and
development and/or inexplicable flashes of genius. At any
moment, some fraction of the capital stock consists of obsolete men and machines which, at some time in the future,
will be replaced by better men and machines. A war, natural disaster, or some sudden pathological alteration in con-

sumer tastes or investor outlook, may occasionally cause the capital stock to decline. But in the usual course of events, the capital stock increases. Barring a nuclear catastrophe or the end of the world through some cosmic disaster, this increase will go on forever. A capital theory that deals with this "reality" can be static only in the sense that it is not concerned with the fascinating problem of how inventions occur. It takes them for granted and tries to show how, in operation with other relevant variables, notably habits of thrift, they affect the economy's rate of income growth.

The difficulties inherent in any effort to marry the idea of capital productivity to the assumption that technology is "given" are perhaps best illustrated by the case of a subsistence economy. In such an economy, total income will presumably increase if additional farm implements appear miraculously—that is, without cost—from the heavens. But this is not what we ought to mean by the proposition that capital is productive. Labor as well as farm implements constitute capital.

The issue is whether total income can be increased by sacrificing consumption in order to build farm implements. If the economy is at the subsistence level, an affirmative answer may not be justified. Any such investment entails the destruction of human capital through starvation, and there is no guarantee that the value of the services made possible by building additional farm implements will exceed the value of the services of the human beings sent to the grave by the investment policy. Clearly, whether income can be increased "eventually" by starving people "now" depends, in large part, upon who is starved—the able-bodied or the very young and very old.

We might note that the only real-world economies for which the assumption that technology is "given" is appropriate have been subsistence economies. In these cases, technical progress, possibly generated within the system but more likely introduced by foreigners, provides the only known road to economic development. To say the obvious, a stone age society does not achieve economic "take-off" by multiplying the number of stone axes.

We might pause here to say one good word for Böhm-Bawerk and Marx. The problem that they faced was real enough: how is it possible to increase income by foregoing consumption in order to construct capital assets? As noted in chapter I, an economist from Mars, untroubled by exposure to the idea of a static state where technology is (allegedly) "given," might urge the obvious answer. Income can be increased by investment because continuous innovation is a fact of life. But Böhm-Bawerk and Marx, as intellectual children of Ricardo, could not bring themselves to discard the postulate of a given technology. Consequently they had no option but to devise some useful myth to explain why capital accumulation is possible. Böhm-Bawerk's myth is that the capital stock can always be increased by lengthening the period of production. Marx's myth is that the application of human labor to inanimate objects mysteriously generates a quantity of surplus value that can take the form of additional capital assets and/or human beings.

Actually, neither Marx nor Böhm-Bawerk ever succeeded in accommodating their thought to a model where technology is given. Much of the time, Böhm-Bawerk's more roundabout method of production is only the new and better machine,[13] and *Das Kapital* abounds with references to the impact of invention on capital accumulation.[14] In

[13] For an excellent elaboration of the truth that the world of Böhm-Bawerk "is neither a stationary nor a fully dynamic world," see L. M. Lachmann, *Capital and Its Structure* (London, 1956), pp. 79–85.

[14] Notably in the long discussion of machinery and modern industry. *Capital*, pp. 365–515.

any event, Böhm-Bawerk and Marx accepted the productivity of investment in capital assets as a fact of life and perceived, however imperfectly, that this productivity influenced both the rate of interest and the rate of capital accumulation. The explicit recognition of this connection may appear to be an intellectual achievement of only modest dimensions. It appears in a more impressive light when one examines the hopelessly confused work of writers who sought to explain interest without any concrete notion of capital productivity.[15]

Capital Theory as Instruction by Analogy

The foregoing discussion has reiterated a proposition first suggested in chapter 1, namely, that capital productivity really has nothing to do with those examples that are usually used to illustrate it—aging wine, breeding rabbits, growing crops, the lathe that can be used to make more lathes, etc. As chapter 1 argued, knowledge is both an input and an output in the production process, and capital accumulation is always associated with the utilization of existing knowledge and the creation of new knowledge. But here the interactions are so fiendishly complex that we are usually content to explain capital accumulation with the aid of analogies.

We dimly perceive that the rate of return on most investments is positive because knowledge is increasing or has recently increased. The wheat crop will be bigger this year

[15] See, for example, C. G. Hoag, *A Theory of Interest* (New York, 1914). Hoag, after explicitly denying the relevance of physical productivity to interest, is reduced to asserting that interest can be earned by investors because people discount future incomes (p. 94). One can, with equal truth, reply that people discount future income because interest can be earned. Hence, Hoag falls back into the pit of circular reasoning from which even the most unconvincing explanation of capital productivity provides an escape.

than last because improved insecticides will be used for the first time. Hopefully, the output of textiles will rise because personnel managers have recently learned new and better ways to screen out unpromising applicants for jobs. The introduction of labor-saving devices will allow a given quantity of cargo to be loaded with fewer man-hours. We can also dimly perceive that arbitrage in the capital market is "tending" to make equal the rates of return on investment in wheat growing, textile manufacture, and cargo loading. But the feat of devising a "realistic" explanation of why investment in wheat yields, say, a 10 percent return (in constant dollars) seems to be beyond us. We make capital productivity intelligible to ourselves by likening it to multiplying rabbits, growing trees, aging wine, etc.[16]

Recapitulation

It is possible to conceive of technical progress—or at any rate, the creation of new knowledge—without capital accumulation. (Research scientists might continue to work on their beloved projects even after the approach of Judgment Day had eliminated all other investment activity.) Many economists believe that they can conceive of capital accumulation without technical progress. In fact, capital accumulation and technical progress always go hand-in-hand

---

[16] For the skeptic who is dissatisfied with all of the explanations of capital productivity discussed in this chapter, there is always resort to mysticism. Thus, Henry George—a better economist than one would infer from the activities of the surviving single taxers who claim intellectual descent from him—despaired of explaining capital productivity and ascribed it to "the active power of nature, the principle of growth, of reproduction, which everywhere characterizes all the forms of that mysterious thing or condition which we call life." *Progress and Poverty* (50th anniversary ed.; New York, 1929), p. 181.

George's attitude is not much different from that of one hard-headed economist who contends that it is sufficient to know that capital is productive; and that there is no point in puzzling over why it is productive.

and this association is perhaps the most important single feature of the investment process.

Given the expansion of knowledge in the recent past, at least one existing capital asset is always of an obsolete type. While it will remain in use for a time, it will not be replaced by an asset of the same obsolete type. Rather the services of the capital stock that could be used to replace it will be used to build a new and better capital asset. The new asset is better in the sense that it provides the same income (in perpetuity) but has a lower construction cost as measured by consumption sacrificed. The addition to income made possible by technical progress can be consumed or invested. Given technical progress, income will increase even though no part of income is invested. Income will increase more rapidly when some part of itself is invested.

The capital productivity that makes possible capital accumulation has nothing to do with the "natural" growth rates of animals and vegetation that are frequently used to illustrate it. Nor is there any good reason to believe that it inheres in the technical superiority of roundabout methods of production over more direct methods. Capital productivity does seem to be inextricably bound up with the creation and utilization of knowledge that is technical progress. Unhappily, the relationship is still extremely obscure and, given the philosophical difficulties involved in explaining change, is probably destined to remain so.

CHAPTER 4

The Marginal Productivity
of Investment

Before the idea of capital productivity can be put to good
use in economic theory, it must be shaped into an instrument of marginal analysis. It is not enough to know that
income can be increased by using the services of existing
capital assets to construct an additional capital asset. We
must know by *how much* income can be increased by the
asset's construction and what relation this extra income
bears to the asset's cost of construction.

Marginal Productivity Defined

Over the years economists have fashioned a number of
very similar instruments of marginal analysis from the
idea of capital productivity. Among them are the rate of
interest in W. S. Jevons, the natural real rate of interest
in Knut Wicksell, the marginal rate of return over cost
in Irving Fisher, the marginal efficiency of capital in
J. M. Keynes, the marginal productivity of investment in
Frank Knight, and the marginal efficiency of investment
in A. P. Lerner.[1] The number of distinguishable analytical
instruments that economists have fashioned from the idea

[1] Jevons, *The Theory of Political Economy* (4th ed.; London, 1911), pp.
244–50; Wicksell, *Lectures on Political Economy*, translated from the third
Swedish edition by E. Classen (2 vols.; London, 1934), II, 192–93; Fisher,
The Theory of Interest (New York, 1930), pp. 158–61; Keynes, *The General
Theory of Employment, Interest, and Money* (London, 1936), pp. 135–46;
Knight, "The Quantity of Capital and the Rate of Interest," *Journal of
Political Economy*, XLIV (1936), 435; Lerner, *The Economics of Control* (New
York, 1944), p. 261.

of capital productivity is much less than the number of labels appended to them, though genuine differences do exist. These differences, however, are unimportant as far as an understanding of basic capital theory goes, and we shall not digress to consider them. The principal purpose of each is the same—to relate the return on an increment of investment to its cost. Let us ignore their differences and call the instrument of marginal analysis that we shall use "the marginal productivity of investment in capital assets." Or, for short, MPI. If this term is awkward, it has the merit of allowing us to start, as far as terminology goes, with a clean slate.

In order to define MPI with precision we must first find a unit of measure that can be applied to capital viewed as a stock and income viewed as a flow of services. This is most easily done with the aid of Frank Knight's Crusonia plant—probably the simplest model ever employed in capital theory.[2] (While the Crusonia plant was named by Knight, its properties were completely, though cryptically, described by W. S. Jevons as early as 1871.)[3]

Let us assume that all human wants are supplied by a species of vegetation that grows at a rate unaffected by human endeavor except as tissue is cut away for consumption. The plant itself is the capital stock. Income is the amount by which the size of the plant would increase, in any time interval, in the absence of consumption. Property consists of rights to consume or invest specified fractions of the Crusonia plant. An economy so favored by nature has only one economic problem. It must decide how much consumption to forego now in order to have more income

[2] "Diminishing Returns from Investment," *Journal of Political Economy*, LII (1944), 29.
[3] *The Theory of Political Economy*, pp. 244-49.

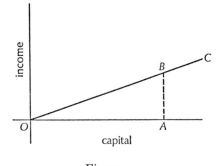

Figure 4.1

later. In this model, MPI is the addition to income produced by an incremental increase in the capital stock
through investment, i.e., by not consuming. Writing Y for
income and K for capital, MPI is $\dfrac{\Delta Y}{\Delta K}$.

Figure 4.1 gives the case where MPI is independent of
the size of the capital stock. Figure 4.2 gives the case where
MPI declines as the capital stock increases, i.e., the case
of diminishing returns to investment. In both figures, income (in perpetuity) is measured along the vertical axis

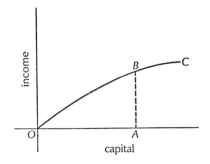

Figure 4.2

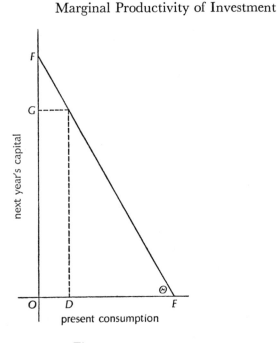

Figure 4.3

and the size of the capital stock along the horizontal axis. In both figures, MPI for a capital stock of size *OA* is given by the slope of the curve *OC* at point *B*.

Figures 4.3 and 4.4 offer an alternative way of representing MPI. In these diagrams *OE* shows the capital stock "now"; *OF* shows what the capital stock will be one year from today if no part of *OE* is consumed now. In order to treat consumption as a stock rather than a flow, we shall posit that all consumption for the time interval is done now. Hence, every point on the curve *EF* represents a possible combination of present consumption and future capital. If, for example, the economy elects to consume *OD* and invest *DE* now, it can have a capital stock

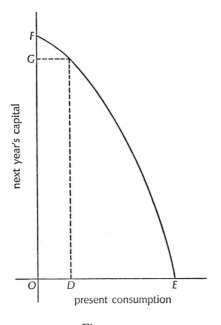

next year's capital

present consumption

Figure 4.4

OG next year. The slope of the curve *EF* at a given point
(-1) gives MPI for the corresponding quantity of investment. In the case of constant returns to investment (figure 4.3), MPI for every quantity of investment is equal to
$\tan \theta - 1$. In the case of diminishing returns to investment
(figure 4.4), there is a different MPI for every different
quantity of investment.

Capital Viewed as Discounted Income

We may profitably pause here to note and fix in mem-
ory, hopefully forever, one feature of the diminishing returns to investment case that has been the source of endless
confusion in capital theory. It is often said that "capital

is income discounted by the rate of interest." It would be more to the point if the supporters of this view defined capital as income discounted by MPI. For arbitrage ensures the equality of MPI and the interest rate, at least in a world where the outcome of every investment can be foretold with perfect certainty.

Suppose that all property consists of rights to consume a portion of a Crusonia plant that grows at the constant rate of 10 percent per annum. Clearly, no investor will loan Crusonia at a rate less than 10 percent. For if he wishes to increase his capital stock, he can do so by not consuming the whole of his income; he secures a 10 percent return on the fraction of income invested. Clearly, also, no investor will pay more than 10 percent to borrow capital assets so long as he has any capital assets of his own. (In a world without investment outlets nobody would make a loan to the man without capital of his own, for if the borrower consumed anything at all, he would be unable to repay the loan in full, even though no interest were charged.)

Even if a man should wish to consume more than his annual income, the cost of consuming a unit of his own capital is only the 10 percent yield sacrificed. Thus there is nothing mysterious about the equality of MPI and the rate of interest on loans of capital assets. It is purely and simply a matter of arbitrage. Any discrepancy between the two rates of return would give rise to a profit that calls forth the transactions that eliminate it. Should MPI exceed the rate of interest, one gains by borrowing other people's capital and investing it. Should the rate of interest exceed MPI, one gains by foregoing direct investment in order to loan capital assets to others.

In a world of free exchange, every owner of capital assets has two ways of adding to his capital stock. He may invest directly by using some part of his income to build additional capital assets. Or he may loan some part of his capital stock to someone else and charge interest on the loan. In a world without risk, the investor has no reason to prefer one way of augmenting his capital stock to the other since they are equally and totally safe. As long as direct investment in capital assets and a loan of capital assets provide the same rate of return, the investor is indifferent between them.

Whether any capital would be borrowed or lent in a world without risk is a moot point. No economic benefits would accrue to borrower or lender in such a world, but then neither would any costs be incurred by either party. We can only say that, if a market for loans of capital assets did exist in a world without risk, the rate of interest would equal MPI.

So far in this book, references to "the rate of interest" have been few and far between. This neglect has not been fortuitous. If the rate of interest is among the terms most frequently used in capital theory, it is also among the most ambiguous and confusing. We shall not, at this time, digress to identify the more popular meanings of the term. This uncongenial task is postponed until chapter 10. For present purposes, it will suffice to note that, in basic capital theory, the rate of interest is a wholly redundant expression. It is a synonym for MPI and signifies nothing else.

Can one say that capital is income discounted by MPI? The unsatisfactory answer must be that *sometimes* capital can be defined in this way. Specifically, capital *is* income discounted by MPI when MPI is independent of the size of the capital stock, i.e., where there are no diminishing returns to investment. Capital *is not* income discounted by MPI when MPI declines as the capital stock increases. The reader is asked to accept on faith for the moment that the two foregoing sentences really do make sense.

Consider figure 4.1. Let the income AB be paid once a year, and let the first payment be due one year from today. The present value of a perpetuity disbursed in this manner is equal to the annual income divided by MPI. In figure 4.1, MPI is AB/OA. Therefore, the present value of AB is $AB/(AB/OA)$ or OA. And the quantity of capital that produced the annual income AB is OA.

Consider now the diminishing returns case given in figure 4.5, which is the same as figure 4.2 except that it contains more information. A capital stock OA yields an income AB. MPI for a capital stock OA is given by the slope of OC at point B; so that when income is discounted by MPI the result is a discounted sum equal to DA.

At first glance, this result is very curious indeed. We know that a capital stock containing OA units of Crusonia produced an income of AB units of Crusonia. But the value of the capital stock is shown to be DA. The conundrum has a simple, though by no means obvious, explanation.

We begin by observing that, if a unit of Crusonia had the power to grow even though detached from the parent plant, there would be no diminishing returns to investment. As soon as diminishing returns set in, the plant would be divided. If diminishing returns were present from the very beginning of growth, the capital stock would consist of a number of infinitely small plants. Therefore, in the Crusonia model, in order to secure diminishing returns to investment we must introduce the following postulate. While any part of the plant can be cut away for consumption, any part of the plant ceases to grow when so cut, and the uncut parent stock continues to

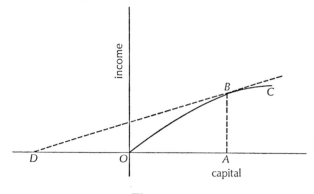

Figure 4.5

grow at a declining rate. The effect of this postulate is, alas, to destroy our one commodity model. We now have an economically significant distinction between "live" and "dead" units of Crusonia. In figure 4.5, *OA* is the quantity of live Crusonia. *DA* is the value of *OA* in terms of dead Crusonia.

In short, when there are diminishing returns to investment, one has need of a *numéraire* even though capital and unconsumed income are a common substance. Note that when capital accumulation takes place subject to diminishing returns, it serves to confer a capital gain on all owners of previously created units of capital.[4] Because MPI has fallen, a given quantity of capital (live Crusonia) now exchanges for a greater quantity of consumable income (dead Crusonia).

We might also note that the above analysis points up a

[4] The difficulty of valuing capital assets under conditions of diminishing returns has not been wholly neglected in capital theory. See A. P. Lerner, "On the Marginal Product of Capital and the Marginal Efficiency of Investment," *Journal of Political Economy*, LXI (1953), 3–4; and T. W. Swan, "Economic Growth and Capital Accumulation," *Economic Record*, XXXII (1956), 352–57.

problem that faces students who seek to measure changes in the "quantity of capital" over time by discounting income. It is not enough to correct for changes in the value of the *numéraire*. Ideally, one must also correct for changes in MPI. If MPI has fallen over time, the estimate of the change in capital obtained by discounting will be too high. If MPI has risen, it will be too low.

Capital Productivity versus Investment Productivity

The Crusonia model allows us to measure changes in the quantity of capital without the need to cast about for a *numéraire* and then construct a price index to measure changes in its purchasing power. One other notable merit of the Crusonia model should be mentioned. Use of the model insures that an increment of investment yields its addition to income "immediately." This feature eliminates the "period of production" and so obviates the need to distinguish between the marginal productivity of capital and the marginal productivity of investment. As we have seen, in the Crusonia model one talks of "the marginal productivity of investment in capital assets" which is simply $\frac{\Delta Y}{\Delta K}$.

Suppose, however, that there is a "period of production" in the sense that an increment of income invested "now" does not begin to yield an addition to the flow of income until "later." On this premise, the marginal productivity of investment is a function of both the marginal productivity of capital and the period of production.

Let $\frac{\Delta Y}{\Delta K}$ denote the marginal productivity of capital, z the marginal productivity of investment, and t the time that must elapse before an investment begins to yield its income,

The marginal productivity of investment is the discount rate which makes the sum of the future incomes made possible by the investment equal to its cost (which is consumption sacrificed). It is this rate which is kept equal by arbitrage to the rate of interest on consumption loans.

When the income resulting from an investment is paid in equal annual installments and the first income payment from an investment made today is due one year from today, the investment may be said to yield its return "immediately" since both pertain to the same accounting period (the year). In this case, the period of production is unity ($t = 1$); and when $n \to \infty$ we write

$$\Delta K = \frac{\Delta Y}{(1 + z)^1} + \frac{\Delta Y}{(1 + z)^2} + \cdots + \frac{\Delta Y}{(1 + z)^n} = \frac{\Delta Y}{z} \quad (1)$$

In equation (1) $z = \dfrac{\Delta Y}{\Delta K}$. But when $t > 1$, the relation of z to $\dfrac{\Delta Y}{\Delta K}$ is given by

$$\Delta K = \Delta Y \left(\frac{1}{z} - \frac{1}{(1 + z)^1} - \cdots - \frac{1}{(1 + z)^{t-1}} \right) \quad (2)$$

Thus, given a period of production greater than unity, the marginal productivity of investment is less than the marginal productivity of capital.

It is tiresome enough to reckon the value of z from the "production function" that relates ΔK to ΔY when $\dfrac{\Delta Y}{\Delta K}$ and t are constants independent of the size of the capital stock K. When $\dfrac{\Delta Y}{\Delta K}$ and t are assumed to vary with K, the task is never attempted. Either z is pulled out of the air on the very reasonable assumption that it "exists"; or $\dfrac{\Delta Y}{\Delta K}$ is used as a proxy for z. The former way of introducing "the marginal productivity of investment" into economic analysis saves a great deal of time, though it is not very useful for making clear the relationship between z and other economic variables. The latter treatment of z is unobjectionable so long as the period of production is "short."

Marginal Productivity and Capital Growth

Before concluding our discussion of marginal productivity we might digress to clear up a minor confusion of long standing in capital theory. Since the first edition of W. S. Jevons' *The Theory of Political Economy* (1871), economists have often equated the rate of interest, and by implication, MPI, with some natural growth rate of the capital stock. This natural growth rate is, by definition, the rate at which the capital stock would grow if consumption were zero. When the length of the investment period is approximately zero, this rate is the maximum attainable "instantaneous" growth rate of the capital stock.

So long as there are constant returns to investment, the identification of MPI with a natural growth rate is valid. In this case, marginal productivity and average productivity are perforce the same thing. Average productivity is always the quotient Y/K. Given constant returns to investment, MPI is also the quotient Y/K (figure 4.1).

In the case of diminishing returns to investment, however, the identification of MPI with a natural growth rate is erroneous. For now, while MPI is a function of the natural growth rate of the capital stock, it is a different magnitude. The average productivity of investment Y/K is the true natural growth rate of the capital stock. Thus in figure 4.5, when the capital stock is OA, the average productivity of investment is AB/OA; the marginal productivity of investment is AB/DA. To repeat: given diminishing returns to investment and continuous growth in the capital stock in the absence of consumption, MPI is a function of the natural growth rate; but it is not equal to this rate.[5] The connection between MPI and capital growth is examined at greater length at the end of this chapter.

Summary

To sum up: If Y denotes income, K denotes capital, and Y is solely a function of K, then the marginal productivity of investment in capital assets is $\dfrac{\Delta Y}{\Delta K}$. The "capital" that has the marginal product ΔY is "real" capital. Only when the marginal productivity of investment is constant can the quantity of real capital be obtained by discounting income.

In the case where the marginal productivity of investment declines as the capital stock increases, complications intrude. Now a unit of consumable income is no longer the same thing as a unit of capital. For while a unit of capital can be used to produce either more capital or consumable income, a unit of consumable income can only be consumed. We have seen that the distinction between capital (live Crusonia) and consumable income (dead Crusonia) is necessary to secure diminishing returns to investment in a model where capital is the only factor of production.

[5] Historically, the practice of equating MPI with the natural growth rate of the capital stock seems to have had two causes. The first was the practice of assuming constant returns to investment in order to simplify the equations needed to show the relation between annual growth and instantaneous growth.

See, for instance, Knight, "The Quantity of Capital and the Rate of Interest," pp. 441–48; or Jevons, *The Theory of Political Economy*, pp. 244–50. The second was the practice of assuming the existence of an interest rate in order to demonstrate that a growing tree will be chopped down when its increase in value becomes equal to the given rate of interest. Fisher, *The Theory of Interest*, pp. 161–70.

When income is divided by the marginal productivity of investment, the result is a figure that gives the value of the capital stock in terms of consumable income. Given diminishing returns to investment, one must learn to live with the distinction between "real capital stock" and the "value of the capital stock." Likewise, one must take care to distinguish MPI and, hence, the rate of interest from the so-called natural growth rate of the real capital stock.

NOTE

Capital Growth, Discount, and Marginal Productivity

A crucial definition. The concept of a "marginal productivity of investment" is the most important single idea in capital theory; yet in most treatments of the subject it is disposed of rather summarily. The temptation is to write Y for income, K for capital stock, $\frac{\Delta Y}{\Delta K}$ for the marginal productivity of investment, and pass on to other matters. As noted, this haste has two unfortunate consequences. It obscures the relation of capital growth to the marginal productivity of investment, and it does not reveal the major pitfall that appears when capital is defined as "income discounted by the marginal productivity of investment."

The case of constant returns. Given constant returns to investment, no serious problems arise when the marginal productivity of investment is to be defined. On this assumption, the capital stock grows at a constant (geometric) rate provided that consumption is zero. The marginal productivity of investment is this "natural" growth rate. It is affected neither by an increase in the capital stock through investment nor by the passing of time. Given constant returns to investment, it is immaterial whether the marginal productivity of investment is defined in terms of annual growth or "instantaneous" growth. We should, however, be clear on the relationship of these two rates.

Let K_0 = the capital stock now

K_t = the capital stock at the end of t years

r = the annual growth rate of the capital stock when consumption is zero

Now suppose the capital stock K_0 to be invested for t years. Then the capital stock at the end of t years K_t is given by

$$K_t = K_0(1 + r)^t \qquad \text{(N1)}$$

Differentiate K_t with respect to t in equation (N1); then,

$$\frac{dK_t}{dt} = K_0(1 + r)^t \log_e (1 + r) \qquad \text{(N2)}$$

When $t \to 0$, $(1 + r)^t \to 1$. Thus,

$$\frac{dK_t}{dt} = K_0 \log_e (1 + r) \qquad \text{(N3)}$$

When $t \approx 0$, $K_t \approx K_0$. Now,

$$\frac{dK}{dt} = K \log_e (1 + r) \qquad \text{(N4)}$$

and

$$\frac{\frac{dK}{dt}}{K} = \log_e (1 + r) \qquad \text{(N5)}$$

Equation (N5) gives the instantaneous, natural growth rate of the capital stock $K = K_0$ when consumption is zero. The marginal productivity of investment is, therefore,

$$\frac{\frac{dK}{dt}}{K} \qquad \text{or} \qquad \log_e (1 + r)$$

For convenience write $p = \log_e (1 + r)$. Now the relation between the annual growth rate r and the instantaneous growth rate p is

$$e^p = (1 + r) \qquad\qquad \text{(N6)}$$

or $\qquad\qquad\qquad r = e^p - 1 \qquad\qquad\qquad \text{(N7)}$

The case of diminishing returns. When there are diminishing returns to investment, the marginal productivity of investment is no longer the natural growth rate of the capital stock. This point deserves emphasis because many authors who use the concept of instantaneous capital growth make one or both of two mistakes. Either they unknowingly assume that there are no diminishing returns to investment, or they assume diminishing returns to investment and mistake the natural growth rate of the capital stock for the rate of interest, i.e., the discount rate. Even the great Wicksell can be charged with this last error.[6]

---

[6] In his famous example of aging wine, Wicksell believed that he had proved that the rate of interest, given diminishing returns to investment, is always greater than the marginal product of capital. But Wicksell begins by accepting Jevons' formula for the rate of interest which makes it "the rate of increase of the produce divided by the whole produce." (In Jevons' notation t is time, Ft is the whole produce, $F't$ is the rate of increase of the produce, and $F't/Ft$ is the rate of interest.)

As we have seen, this formula gives the rate of interest only when there are no diminishing returns to investment. Consequently, Wicksell goes wrong from the start by equating the rate of interest with the *average* productivity of investment. What he proves is that, given diminishing returns, the average productivity of investment is greater than the marginal productivity of investment. *Lectures on Political Economy*, I, 178–81. See also L. A. Metzler, "The Rate of Interest and the Marginal Product of Capital," *Journal of Political Economy*, LVIII (1950), 289–306.

Let p = the instantaneous rate of increase in the capital stock when consumption is zero

K = the capital stock

Y = "instantaneous" income

m = the marginal productivity of investment

Let the relation between p and K be given by

$$p = a - bK \qquad \text{(N8)}$$

where $a \geq 1,\ 0 < b < 1$.

By definition,

$$Y = Kp \qquad \text{(N9)}$$

and

$$m = \frac{dY}{dK} \qquad \text{(N10)}$$

Equation (N9) can be written

$$Y = aK - bK^2 \qquad \text{(N11)}$$

Differentiating Y with respect to K in equation (N11) and substituting m for $\frac{dY}{dK}$, we have

$$m = a - 2bK \qquad \text{(N12)}$$

Let V denote the "discounted" value of the (perpetual) income Y. Then

$$V = \frac{Y}{m} \qquad \text{(N13)}$$

$$K = \frac{Y}{p} \qquad \text{(N9)}$$

$$p > m \qquad \text{(N8, 11)}$$

$$V > K \qquad \text{(N14)}$$

Once again we have the result that we first obtained with the aid of geometry. Given diminishing returns to investment, and only one factor of production, "capital" and "income" are two different things even though income is the "harvest" of capital and capital yields only one "product." To secure diminishing returns in this model, it is necessary to posit that an increment of consumption ceases to grow the moment it is cut away from the parent capital stock. Otherwise diminishing returns could be evaded by dividing the capital stock whenever they threatened to materialize. Thus a unit of consumption still invested in the capital stock has a greater value than a unit already harvested; the former can still grow, the latter cannot.

To summarize: Given diminishing returns to investment and a single factor of production, the "quantity of capital," or "capital stock" as this book has usually called it, is not "income discounted by the marginal productivity of investment." For, on these assumptions, "capital" and "income" are necessarily different commodities. The discount process gives the value of capital stock in terms of consumable income.

CHAPTER 5   The Taste for Investment

In chapter 3 we noted that early discussions of the nature and necessity of interest were confused by much circular reasoning because the participants did not clearly distinguish between capital productivity and the taste factor that also affects capital accumulation. At various times, this taste factor has been termed, among other things, abstinence, waiting, time-preference, impatience, thrift. We shall call it simply "the taste for investment." The new label is introduced for two reasons: first, to avoid identifying our formulation of the concept with certain unsatisfactory formulations in the past, and second, to place the emphasis where it belongs, i.e., on capital accumulation or investment.

The Taste for Investment Described

By the taste for investment we shall mean simply the willingness of an individual to exchange present consumption for capital assets. When this exchange is made, the individual may be trading some quantity of present consumption for some (presumably) greater quantity of future consumption. But this need not be the case. The income resulting from investment can itself be invested in whole or in part.

Historically, economists have debated at length the question: Does abstinence, waiting, etc., influence the rate of interest? We shall give this ancient controversy short shrift. What we shall call the taste for investment affects the rate of interest if, and only if, the marginal productivity of in-

vestment (MPI) falls as the capital stock increases.[1] Axiomatically the taste for investment affects the rate of
capital accumulation irrespective whether MPI rises, falls,
or remains constant as the capital stock increases. This
truth will be elaborated in the next chapter.

In order to formulate the taste for investment with
precision we must take care to disentangle it from MPI
and the taste for risk. The taste for investment influences
the economy's preference for future income over present consumption—what Irving Fisher and many others
have called time-preference. But MPI and the taste for
risk also influence the preference for future income over
present consumption.

Assume that it is possible to invest present consumption
and so obtain additional income beginning at some time
in the future. Then, the greater MPI, the greater the cost
of not investing present consumption, that is, the greater
the amount of future income sacrificed. This truth we
have met already on several occasions, and since Fisher
wrote, most economists in treating capital theory have
carefully distinguished between "the impatience to spend
income and the opportunity to invest it."

Fisher, however, made impatience—his later name for
positive time-preference—depend upon both the taste for
investment and the taste for risk (though he did not use
this nomenclature) with confusing results.[2] He correctly

[1] The above truth was expressed clearly, if not forcefully, by Friedrich
Hayek: "Time-preference is a subordinate factor compared with the productivity of investment in determining the rate of interest, since it operates only
by way of determining the rate of savings and the rate of capital accumulation, and hence the productivity of investment. In the short run, it merely
adapts itself to the given marginal productivity of investment." *The Pure
Theory of Capital* (London, 1941), p. 413.

[2] *The Rate of Interest* (New York, 1907), pp. 99–102, 207–20; *The Theory
of Interest* (New York, 1930), pp. 76–80.

My own prejudice is that Fisher's hybrid concept of time-preference has

emphasized that the preference for present consumption over future income is influenced by the amount of risk associated with investment and the willingness of investors to accept it. Assuming that the economy has an aversion to risk in that most investors will not bear it unless they are paid to do so, the greater the amount of risk involved, the stronger the preference for present consumption over future income. Nevertheless, the taste for investment and the taste for risk are two different things.

Even though the outcome of every investment could be known with perfect certainty, the economy would have to decide what fraction of income to invest. Even though all investment outcomes were known in the sense that probability coefficients could be assigned to them, attitudes toward risk could still affect the fraction of income invested. Our discussion of risk is reserved for chapter 10. Here it will suffice to say that the taste for risk affects investment to the extent that a cost must be incurred to pool individual investments and so afford insurance against loss to individual investors, and to the extent that a cost must be incurred to organize lotteries. As we shall see, the connection between lotteries and investment is not really farfetched. The man who delights in risk taking may indulge either by investing or participating in a lot-

---

outlived its usefulness and should be discarded. It is impossible to say what the rate of interest would be in a market unaffected by any influence except the desires of individuals to consume now rather than later, i.e., in a world where no investment is possible and all risks (including the risk of unanticipated death) could be avoided without cost. Fisher believed that time-preference was always positive and, hence, that the rate of interest must always be positive. But in such a world a negative rate of interest would seem to be equally plausible. For the view that Fisher's concept of time-preference is worth polishing and perfecting, see T. C. Koopmans, "Stationary Ordinal Utility and Impatience," *Econometrica*, XXVIII (1960), 287–309.

tery, so that these two activities are rival forms of gambling whose returns tend to be kept equal by arbitrage.

An Application of Indifference Curve Analysis

The Crusonia model employed in the preceding chapter allows us to describe the taste for investment independently of MPI and risk. In figure 5.1, the vertical axis gives the assured income in perpetuity that will begin some time in the future; the horizontal axis gives consumption now. Present consumption can be expressed as so many units of Crusonia. Income can be expressed as so many units of Crusonia per unit of time.

Curves I_1I_1', I_2I_2', and I_3I_3' are three of the infinitely large number of community indifference curves that can be drawn.[3] Any combination of present consumption and future income represented by a point on I_3I_3' is preferred to any combination represented by a point on I_2I_2' or I_1I_1'.[4] This is only to say that the economy is indifferent between combinations of present consumption and income represented by points on the same indifference curve. The slope of each curve declines as it falls away to the right.

[3] The application of indifference curve analysis to capital theory was, like so many other innovations, the work of Fisher. *The Rate of Interest* (New York, 1907), p. 387. Fisher, however, never related income (in perpetuity) to the capital stock in his diagrams. The geometry of figures 5.1, 5.2, and 5.3 is based more directly upon a recent modification of Fisher. Wassily Leontief, "Theoretical Note on Time-Preference, Productivity of Capital, Stagnation, and Economic Growth," *American Economic Review*, XLVIII (1958), 105–11.

[4] Some authors have denied the possibility of constructing community indifference curves that do not intersect on the ground that "allocating the same totals differently among people must generally change the resulting equilibrium price ratio." P. A. Samuelson, "Social Indifference Curves," *Quarterly Journal of Economics*, LXX (1956), 5. This objection does not apply to a model that produces only one commodity and in which the rate of interest cannot diverge from the marginal productivity of investment. In such a model, the rate of interest which gives the terms on which present consumption can be exchanged for future income is the only "price."

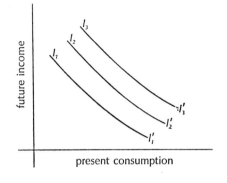

Figure 5.1

Hence the economy's marginal rate of substitution of income for present consumption declines as present consumption increases.

Figure 5.1 describes the economy in which the economy's preference for present consumption over future income is not affected by an increase in economic welfare. Should we posit that the inhabitants become increasingly thrifty as present consumption and income are increased by the same proportion, a new set of indifference curves is needed. It is provided by figure 5.2. Here we note that, when growing wealth is associated with increasing thrift, each successively higher indifference curve is flatter than the last, that is, as wealth increases, the economy is prepared to sacrifice an increasing quantity of present consumption to secure a given quantity of future income. Conversely, when growing wealth is associated with decreasing thrift, each successively higher indifference curve becomes steeper than the last. This latter possibility is depicted in figure 5.3.

Figures 5.1, 5.2, 5.3 allow us to establish a taste for investment that is independent of the marginal productivity of investment and the risk associated with investment.

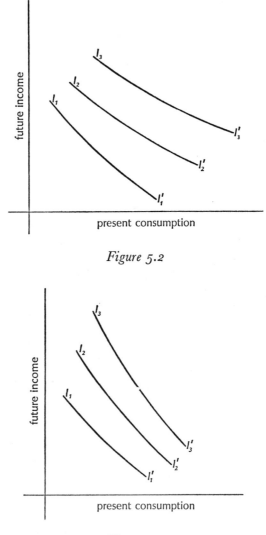

Figure 5.2

Figure 5.3

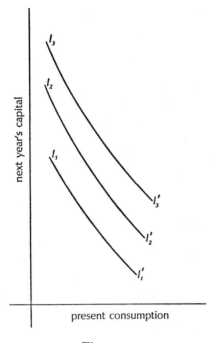

Figure 5.4

These diagrams, however, are difficult to use in conjunction with information on the marginal productivity of investment because future income is a flow and present consumption is a stock. Fortunately, this complication can be circumvented by a simple change in our geometry.

In figure 5.4 the vertical axis represents the stock of real capital at the beginning of next year; the horizontal axis again represents capital available for consumption now. All combinations of present consumption and future capital represented by points on curve I_3I_3' are equally desirable. Any combination on I_3I_3' is preferred to every combination

on I_2I_2' or I_1I_1'. We shall have occasion to use the indifference curves of figure 5.4 in the next chapter.

An Objection to Indifference Curves Considered

We might digress to note that the use of indifference
curves in capital theory implies a view of the investment
process that has not gone unchallenged. This view assumes
that economic growth involves an unending sequence of
choices between consumption and investment. An investment decision is presumed to be made "now" for some
interval of time that extends but a little way into the future.
At a later date, another investment decision will presumably be made for another finite interval of time and
so *ad infinitum*.

Nobody would deny that, in the real world, investment
decisions are made in this way—they do constitute an unending sequence of choices. Some economists, however,
question whether this view of the investment process is
compatible with the assumption made in elementary capital
theory that "investors have perfect foresight." By their
view, when investors are so equipped, the investment
horizon extends not from "now" to "next year" but rather
from now to infinity, hence any investment decision made
now must seek to maximize the "flow of all future utilities"
until the end of time.[5] In effect, economists who reject the
use of indifference curves in capital theory argue that the
course of future economic growth is to be regarded as being
determined for all time in a single grand decision.

For my own part, I find this objection to indifference
curves unconvincing. A postulate that gives investors per-

[5] See, for example, F. M. Westfield, "Time-Preference and Economic
Growth," *American Economic Review*, XLIV (1959), 1037–41.

fect foresight in the near future raises enough difficult issues of methodology.[6] A postulate that gives investors perfect knowledge of all future history is total nonsense. And once the decision is made in capital theory to treat the investment decision as relating to some finite interval of time, the objection to indifference curves considered above is seen to be without foundation. The finite interval for which the investment decision is made can, of course, be as long or as short as one cares to make it.[7]

Recapitulation

We are now in a position to sum up our findings on the two fundamental ideas of capital theory—capital productivity and the taste for investment. The marginal productivity of investment gives the terms on which capital can be accumulated or consumed, the cost of investment being the consumption that must be sacrificed to make it. The taste for investment is a statement of the economy's willingness to pay this cost when one has allowed for the effects

[6] The principal objection to assuming that any part of the future is known with perfect certainty has been cogently given by Frank Knight: "Any rigorous exclusion of uncertainty from economic activity, even under the most unprogressive conditions, not only is unrealistic but is ultimately a contradiction in terms. . . . Ultimately, we confront the paradox that perfectly economic behavior is not economic behavior at all; apart from the possibility of error, it would not be motivated but would be simply a mechanical response to a situation." "Diminishing Returns from Investment," *Journal of Political Economy*, LII (1944), 41.

[7] In analyzing the investment decision, one can dispense with indifference curves without the sacrifice of precision provided that more complicated utility functions are put in their place. See F. P. Ramsey, "A Mathematical Theory of Saving," *Economic Journal*, XXXVIII (1928), 543–59; P. A. Samuelson and R. M. Solow, "A Complete Capital Model Involving Heterogeneous Capital Goods," *Quarterly Journal of Economics*, LXX (1956), 537–62.

An alternative treatment of investment based on Ramsey's article is presented in Appendix A.

of risk, and investor attitudes toward risk, on the investment decision. In fine, capital productivity is a matter of technology. The taste for investment is perforce a matter of taste.

CHAPTER 6   Equilibrium

in Capital Theory

We have now examined the two fundamental ideas in capital theory—capital productivity and the taste for investment. In our examination, we employed what is probably the simplest model of economic growth ever devised— Frank Knight's Crusonia plant—to make clear the meaning of "the marginal productivity of investment in capital assets" (MPI). The taste for investment was obtained by deleting the taste for risk from Irving Fisher's concept of time-preference.

Constant Returns to Investment

Let us now demonstrate how capital productivity and the taste for investment interact to determine simultaneously MPI, the rate of interest on loans of capital assets, the growth rate of the capital stock, the growth rate of income, and the division of income between investment and consumption. Once again the Crusonia model is used to simplify the exposition. Indeed, henceforth the Crusonia model will serve as our principal frame of reference since it admirably permits us to concentrate on fundamentals.[1]

[1] In the literature of capital theory Knight's Crusonia plant has many close substitutes. One recent addition is Professor Samuelson's "surrogate capital"—a homogeneous capital jelly which can be transformed without cost into any sort of consumption good or capital good. Unlike the Crusonia plant, surrogate capital, in the absence of consumption, will grow only when a dash of labor is added. Hence, Samuelson's model is condemned from the outset to the complications of two factor production and diminishing returns to investment. "Parable and Realism in Capital Theory: The

As a pedagogical device, it has two outstanding merits.

First, it allows us to ignore (for the most part) the various "periods of production" that so greatly complicate the task of setting forth the essentials of capital theory without contributing to the clarification of any important truth. In the absence of consumption, the Crusonia plant grows continuously, hence, a capital asset—that is, a unit of Crusonia—has no period of gestation. Likewise, if consumption occurs continuously, the income of a capital asset has no meaningful period of production. We shall presently posit that all consumption takes place on one day of the year and so introduce a period of production for consumable income into the analysis. But this postulate is a pedagogical artifice that allows the substitution of simple geometry for simple calculus.

Second, use of the Crusonia model allows us to escape the always vexing problem of measurement. Now capital, income, consumption, and investment can all be expressed as so many units of Crusonia, and changes in these magnitudes can be expressed quantitatively in terms of the basic Crusonia unit of measurement. This advantage of the Crusonia model should not be underestimated. Once a second commodity is introduced into an economic model, one must select one of the commodities to serve as a *numéraire* to express the values of capital, income, consumption, and investment. If, as a result of capital accumulation, the output of one commodity increases faster than the output of the other, the value of the *numéraire* will change.

Surrogate Production Function," *Review of Economic Studies*, XXIX, No. 3 (1962), 193–206.

For an intriguing variation on Samuelson's model where income is "putty" until it is invested and thereafter "hard-baked clay," see E. S. Phelps, "Substitution, Fixed Proportions, Growth, and Distribution," *International Economic Review*, IV (1963), 265–88.

When the value of the *numéraire* changes, one must construct a price index in order to estimate "real" changes in capital, income, consumption, and investment. Various price indices are possible; none is indisputably the right one, and, in any accounting period, the change that is registered in "real" economic magnitudes will depend upon the particular price index chosen.

Let us again posit that, although the Crusonia plant grows continuously, each year all consumption takes place on a given day. The introduction of this assumption allows us to treat consumption as a stock rather than a flow, and hence to represent consumption and the capital stock on the same axis. The economy has only one economic decision to make. Once a year it must decide how much of the Crusonia plant to consume. The more Crusonia consumed "now," the smaller the plant that will be available for consumption and/or investment next year.

Figure 6.1 incorporates the indifference curves and investment schedule developed in the last two chapters. Since the investment schedule CF is a straight line, there are no diminishing returns to investment. Present consumption is measured along the horizontal axis; the capital stock (Crusonia) that will be available one year from now is measured along the vertical axis. If we assume that it is technically possible to consume all capital "now" in one grand orgy, then the distance OC measures both the maximum possible consumption and the present stock of capital assets. If the economy elects to consume the amount OB now, its capital stock will fall to BC but grow back to OH by the end of the year. In figure 6.1, OH is equal to OC. Therefore, OB is the annual income of the capital stock BC. If consumption is less than OB, the stock of capital assets will be greater at the start of next year than

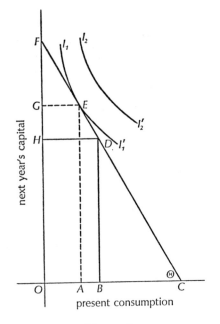

Figure 6.1

now—the economy "saves" or "invests" income. If consumption is greater than OB, then the stock of capital
assets will be less at the start of next year—the economy
dissaves or disinvests by consuming capital.

Since there are constant returns to investment, each
successive unit of consumption foregone brings the same
addition to capital stock. Thus the marginal productivity
of investment (MPI) is always equal to $\tan \theta - 1$. It is
also equal to $(OF/OC) - 1$ and to HF/OH. We perceive
then that when MPI is a constant, MPI is the rate at
which the capital stock would grow if consumption were
zero. From figure 6.1, it is apparent that the economy
attains its highest indifference curve I_1I_1' by consuming

OA now and investing AC in order to have a capital stock OG at the beginning of next year. For a period of one year,

$OC = OH =$ initial capital stock
$OG =$ final capital stock
$OA = GE =$ actual consumption
$AB =$ consumable income invested
$HG =$ growth in capital stock ("net investment")

$\dfrac{HG}{OH} =$ growth rate of capital stock

$\dfrac{AB}{OB} =$ fraction of income invested

$\dfrac{AC}{OC} =$ fraction of capital stock invested

Figure 6.1 depicts the "normal" case of an economy that adds to its capital stock during the year. To derive a zero growth rate we need only revise our diagram to make the indifference curve I_1I_1' tangent to the line CF at point D. For at this point of tangency, the economy would maximize economic welfare by consuming all of its income OB. To show capital consumption we would make the point of tangency lie somewhere between points D and C.

Diminishing Returns to Investment: The Short Run

Our geometry is easily revised to accommodate the case where MPI declines as the capital stock increases. In figure 6.2 the quantity of *capital* invested now is AC while the quantity of *income* invested now is AB. During the year the capital stock will rise by HG to OG. Therefore, the average rate of return on capital invested is equal to $(OG/AC) - 1$ while the average rate of return on income invested is $(HG/AB) - 1$. Note that both of these average

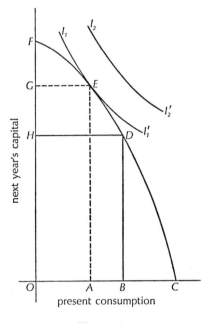

Figure 6.2

rates are above average MPI which is given by the slope
of *FC* at point *E* (−1).

Here we might delay for a moment to reiterate two important truths encountered in chapter 4. First, the rate of
interest on loans of capital assets is tied by arbitrage to
MPI. Indeed, the equality of the rate of interest and MPI
is implied by the proposition that the economy has achieved
its highest indifference curve; so that in figure 6.2 the
annual rate of interest is equal to the slope of *CF* at point *E*
(−1). Second, when MPI declines as the capital stock
increases, the value of the capital stock obtained by dividing annual income by the rate of interest is always greater
than the real capital stock.

As we have found, there can be no diminishing returns in the Crusonia model unless a unit of the vegetation ceases to grow once it is cut away from the parent plant. When this happens, 10 units of harvested or "dead" Crusonia will exchange for something less than 10 units of "live" Crusonia not yet detached from the parent plant. On these terms, nobody will harvest a unit of Crusonia unless he means to consume it. Given diminishing returns to investment, the marginal productivity of investment is always less than the average productivity of investment in our model. By definition, the real capital stock is income divided by the average productivity of investment. By definition, the value of the capital stock is income divided by the marginal productivity of investment.

Equilibrium Capital Stock versus Equilibrium Capital Growth

Does the analysis that we have developed so far imply an equilibrium capital stock or merely an equilibrium path of growth in the capital stock? We have it on Frank Knight's authority that the notion of an equilibrium capital stock so often employed in economic theory is thoroughly pernicious since it distracts attention from that feature of the capital stock most worthy of study—its continuous growth.[2] Perhaps so. Our analysis, however, indicates that an equilibrium capital stock and an equilibrium rate of growth for the capital stock are both logical possibilities. Which of these two possibilities will be realized depends upon two things—the presence or absence of diminishing

[2] According to Knight, "ordinary or normal-equilibrium price analysis has no application to a situation of the type presented by the capital market" because "in the only world of which we have any knowledge as a basis for discussing interest theory, or with respect to which we have any reason for doing so, the total investment of capital is always increasing." "The Quantity of Capital and the Rate of Interest: Part II," *Journal of Political Economy,* XLIV (1936), 614.

returns to investment and the map of the economy's taste
for investment.

Consider first the case of constant returns to investment
(figure 6.1). If the economy is already choosing to invest
part of its income—and if the taste for investment is not
altered by growing wealth—then the capital stock grows
forever at a constant rate. Recall that the taste for investment is not altered by growing wealth if the economy's
indifference curves all have the same elasticities for each
quantity of present consumption as in figure 6.1. When
growing wealth is associated with an increasing taste for
investment—when capital accumulation raises the "marginal propensity to save"—the capital stock grows forever. Moreover, on these two assumptions—a constant
MPI and an increasing taste for investment—the capital
stock grows at an increasing rate until ultimately all income is invested. The growth rate of the capital stock then
becomes equal to MPI.

If one begins by positing a constant MPI and positive
savings out of income, an equilibrium capital stock can
come about in only one way. The economy must become
increasingly spendthrift as its income is raised by investment; so that there finally comes a day when the whole of
income is consumed. Thus, while an equilibrium capital
stock and a constant MPI are formally compatible, the
juxtaposition is most unlikely. One may believe with
J. M. Keynes that the habit of thrift (a virtue or vice
depending upon the economy's approximation to full employment) is encouraged by growing wealth.[3] Or one may
doubt with Milton Friedman that the habit of thrift is

[3] *The General Theory of Employment, Interest, and Money* (New York, 1936),
pp. 113–31.

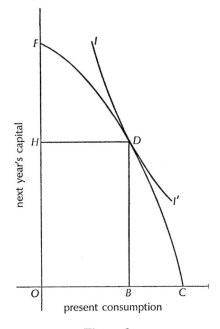

Figure 6.3

significantly affected by growing wealth.[4] As yet, however, nobody has seriously argued that growing wealth reduces the willingness to save.

Consider now the case of diminishing returns to investment. If the economy is already investing part of its present income—and if its taste for investment is not affected by growing wealth—then an equilibrium capital stock will ultimately be reached. The case of long-run equilibrium is described by figure 6.3 where the economy achieves its highest indifference curve by consuming the whole of its

[4] *A Theory of the Consumption Function* (Princeton, 1957), especially pp. 20–37.

income OB. Should the taste for investment be increased by growing wealth, capital formation goes on forever, albeit at an ever-declining rate. It approaches that limit given by the size of the capital stock at which MPI is equal to zero.

In fine, a constant MPI does not necessarily imply a continuous increase in the capital stock. Nor does a declining MPI imply an equilibrium capital stock. Capital accumulation depends upon the taste for investment as well as upon the productivity of investment.

Equilibrium with Ultimate Bliss

Before concluding our discussion of equilibrium in capital theory, we might note a logical possibility that has received the attention of economists and hardly anybody else. Conceivably, consumers can become sated with the services of capital assets before MPI has fallen to zero. (Not that consumers will necessarily be sated with these services, i.e., income, even if MPI does reach zero; satiation with an MPI exactly equal to zero would be an astounding coincidence.) This happy condition can be viewed as "ultimate bliss." (The finer points of bliss are discussed in Appendix A.) Should ultimate bliss be achieved, consumption perforce becomes constant since no more is desired on any terms. What happens to investment when ultimate bliss has been achieved is not so clear.

In our Crusonia case, investment consists entirely of not consuming, so that when ultimate bliss has been achieved, investment will increase. Indeed, now every addition to income resulting from investment is itself immediately invested. In the more realistic case where investment involves the irksome necessity of constructing machines and training human beings, investment will presumably cease when ultimate bliss has been achieved.

Diminishing Returns to Investment: The Long Run

Everyone in his first course in economics learns to distinguish between a price change resulting from movement along a supply (or demand) curve and a price change resulting from a shift in the curve itself. The student of capital theory should exercise similar caution. He will thereby avoid the error of distinguished economists who have reasoned that, since the rate of interest shows no unmistakable tendency to decline over the years, there are no demonstrable diminishing returns to investment.

When, as in the real world, capital assets are specialized to a few uses, there are undoubtedly diminishing returns to investment. If the rate of interest has not fallen in the last two hundred years, the correct inference is, for once, the obvious one: there is some force at work which is continually raising the MPI schedule. While this force has been given many names, it is most commonly called technical progress or the growth of knowledge.

Strictly speaking, investment has two dimensions—magnitude and duration. So far in this book the first has been emphasized. Writing Y for income and K for capital stock, we have equated the marginal productivity of investment with dY/dK on the assumption that an increase in income cannot come about except through an increase in the capital stock. In a world of technical change this is manifestly not true. A "realistic" view of diminishing returns is afforded by figure 6.4. Here capital is measured along the X plane, income along the Y plane, and time along the Z plane. At any moment, there are diminishing returns to

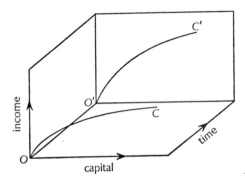

Figure 6.4

investment. Also, at any moment, the MPI schedule is shifting upward. Hence, the increase in income (dY) is a function of both size of the capital stock K and the moment in time T at which the investment is made.

A little reflection on figure 6.4 will serve to clear up a very troublesome obscurity in capital theory. Older economists were fond of debating the question: Would capital accumulation and the growth of income cease if the rate of interest fell to zero? (By the rate of interest they usually meant the marginal productivity of investment.) If income is solely a function of the quantity of capital employed, the answer is clearly yes. If, however, technical change is constantly raising the marginal productivity of investment, the answer is just as clearly no. Given continuous technical change, a marginal productivity of investment equal to zero merely signifies that the rate of income growth cannot be increased by additional savings out of income.

Here we can profitably resort to the Crusonia analogy once more. Suppose that at every moment the growth rate of the Crusonia plant varies inversely with its size—the bigger plant grows more slowly than the smaller plant.

But suppose also that at every moment a continuous flow of benign mutations is raising the natural growth rate of every size of plant by the same percentage. In this situation plant growth is maximized by carrying investment—that is, by restricting consumption—to the point where the marginal productivity of investment is zero.

From the pedagogical point of view, the case for limiting the exposition of capital theory to the model that gives constant returns to investment is overwhelming. The pitfalls that lie in wait for one who seeks to expound capital theory on the assumption that there are diminishing returns to investment are many and painful. Several we have already noted, but one other should be mentioned. When we use a diminishing returns to investment model, it is necessary to specify whether "income" is perishable, storable with cost, or storable without cost. For storing present income and adding to the capital stock by investment are alternative ways of increasing future consumption.[5] When the object is clear exposition, the advantages of sticking to a model where the marginal productivity of investment is a constant can hardly be overestimated.

The Taste for Investment and the Interest Rate

Before concluding our preliminary remarks on the rate of interest, we might note that our analysis has resolved a venerable and acrimonious controversy in capital theory. In a world without risk, the rate of interest is kept equal to MPI by arbitrage. MPI is a matter of technology and not of taste. Can we therefore say that writers who, following Frank Knight, insist that the taste for investment has nothing to do with the determination of the rate of

[5] The economics of storage, and their relevance to the investment decision, are briefly considered in chapter 12.

interest are correct? These writers are wholly correct provided that two conditions are fulfilled: there are no diminishing returns to investment, i.e., MPI is a constant; and the outcome of every investment is completely predictable.

When MPI is constant, sure, and certain, the taste for investment will influence the fraction of income that the economy wishes to save. But MPI will not itself be affected by this decision. If there are diminishing returns to investment—if MPI declines as the capital stock grows—the advocates of capital productivity theories of interest are only partly correct. For now the taste for investment influences the rate at which the capital stock grows. And the rate at which MPI declines is a function of the rate at which the capital grows. In short, an exposition of capital theory that relates the rate of interest to capital productivity always contains a portion of truth. An exposition that relates the rate of interest to the taste for investment contains a portion of truth whenever diminishing returns to investment are implicitly or explicitly assumed.

The assumption that investment is associated with risk introduces a number of complications into capital theory that deserve a treatment of their own. We shall meet them in chapter 10. It will suffice here to anticipate our discussion of risk with two assertions. The willingness of individual investors to invest is influenced by their taste for risk. And changing attitudes toward risk can affect the rate of interest—or, more accurately, the *rates* of interest—even though there are constant returns to investment "in general." The connection between investment and interest rates is more complicated than appears at first glance.

CHAPTER 7   Returns to Investment

The Crusonia model employed in the preceding two chapters is an admirable pedagogical device for making clear what we mean by "the marginal productivity of investment in capital assets" and "a taste for investment." When the object is to set forth, in an easily memorized form, the relationships among consumption, investment, capital growth, income growth, and the rate of interest, the Crusonia model has no rivals. Still, an exposition of capital theory via the Crusonia model is instruction by analogy, and while the use of analogies probably cannot be avoided in capital theory, any particular analogy should not be pushed too far.

The Problem of Diminishing Returns

Over the years economists have often debated whether, *ceteris paribus*, a decrease in MPI must always accompany an increase in the capital stock. That is, are there diminishing returns to investment? If not, why not? The Crusonia model can throw little light on this problem. When a constant rate of growth for the all-purpose vegetation is assumed, we have constant returns to investment. When a decreasing rate of growth is assumed, we have diminishing returns to investment.

According to all versions of capital theory, the accumulation of capital assets is possible because investment in capital assets is "productive." By foregoing the consumption of some part of its income an economy can add to its stock of capital assets. In chapters 1 and 3, we traced capital productivity to the continuous, unending growth of knowledge about production possibilities. This growth insures that, at any given moment, at least one asset in the capital stock is obsolete. (We have seen that, by definition, an obsolete capital asset is one which will be replaced by a "better" capital asset when it is fully depreciated, i.e., when its contribution to variable costs is no longer covered by its contribution to total revenue.) We did not categorically deny that an economy could add to its capital stock even though technology is "given." This possibility, however, was found to be not worth exploring given the absence of real-world instances of capital accumulation without technical progress.

Chapter 4 made use of the Crusonia model to define the marginal productivity of investment in capital assets (MPI). Given constant returns to investment, MPI is the rate at which the capital stock would grow if consumption were zero. Given diminishing returns to investment, MPI is a function of the instantaneous rate at which the capital stock would grow if consumption were zero. MPI is equal to both the rate of interest on loans of capital assets and the rate at which future income is discounted. Thus the natural growth rate of the Crusonia model affects consumption and investment in much the same way as the natural growth rate of the real-world capital stock that inheres in the growth of knowledge.

Unhappily, while the Crusonia model is well suited to make clear the meaning of MPI, it cannot throw light on the forces which, in the real world, determine MPI. Specifically, it cannot help us to grasp the leading issues of that most acrimonious and confused of controversies: are there diminishing returns to investment?

My own prejudice is that this question is not worth the time and effort that has been expended in trying to answer it. Technical progress is continuous, unending, and by far the most powerful force causing the stock of capital assets to grow. Certainly, as John Rae long ago observed, there is nothing "in the appearance of human affairs which should induce us to conclude that the increase of the national capital ever does, in fact, proceed, unless in conjunction with some successful effort of the inventive faculty, some improvement of some of the employments formerly practiced in the community, or some discovery of new arts."[1]

Therefore, the exposition of capital theory can, without violence to reality, proceed on the assumption that there are no diminishing returns to investment "in the long run." (One could, of course, with equal justification assume that, in any accounting period, there is no certain relationship between capital accumulation and MPI; that, depending upon the growth of knowledge and its cost, MPI may rise, fall, or remain unchanged.)

Nevertheless, most of the influential expositions of capital theory over the years have posited a static state where the stock of "natural agents" and the knowledge of production possibilities is given. Many of them have reached the conclusion that, within this context, capital accumulation is subject to diminishing returns. Indeed, the idea of diminishing returns to investment occupies so large a place in the history of capital theory that we must digress to examine it—if only to arm ourselves against error. There are, in fact, two different arguments which assert that, in

[1] *Statement of Some New Principles on the Subject of Political Economy, Exposing the Fallacies of the System of Free Trade, and of Some Other Doctrines Maintained in the "Wealth of Nations"* (Boston, 1834), p. 22.

the static state, investment is subject to diminishing returns. The first is wholly specious; the second, while open to objection as usually formulated, does make a minor contribution to an understanding of the investment process.

Diminishing Returns in the Single Investment

So far as the creation of a particular type of capital asset is concerned, there are obviously diminishing returns to investment. The demand for a capital asset is derived from the demand for the service that it will provide during its lifetime. When the amount of service offered increases, the price of the service will fall and, with it, the rate of return on investment in this type of capital asset. It matters not whether a given type of capital asset is produced under conditions of increasing, decreasing, or constant cost as measured by the physical units of other types of assets that must be sacrificed to produce it. By itself, a negatively inclined demand curve for the service of the particular type of asset insures diminishing returns to investment in that type.

Early writers on capital theory who perceived the existence of diminishing returns to a certain type of investment allowed themselves to fall victim to the fallacy of composition. From the "fact" that every type of investment when viewed in isolation is subject to diminishing returns, they inferred that diminishing returns must characterize the same set of investments when all are increased simultaneously.[2] Clearly, this inference is invalid.[3] In the single

[2] See, for example, T. N. Carver, *The Distribution of Wealth* (New York, 1904), p. 254, where the reader is assured that "it is hardly necessary to state that anything which increases the spirit of thrift, frugality, and foresight will reduce the marginal sacrifice of abstinence, and correspondingly increase the supply of capital and reduce the rate of interest."

[3] This particular fallacy of composition persisted in capital theory long after it was exposed. As early as 1836 Nassau Senior pointed out that, for

investment, diminishing returns are required by the existence of an eventually negatively inclined demand curve
for the services yielded by that investment. Yet, for all
investments taken together, "supply creates its own demand;" so that it is meaningless to speak of a negatively
inclined demand curve for capital assets in general. The
case for diminishing returns to investment, if it exists,
must rest upon some other foundation.

Diminishing Returns with a Fixed Factor of Production

A more common version of the case for diminishing
returns to investment is based upon the distinction between
capital and other "factors of production." (This distinction
we assumed away in chapter 2.) Strictly speaking, this
version is merely "the law of variable proportions" in different guise. It asserts that if production of income requires the use of capital in combination with other factors,
and the supply of the other factors is fixed and unalterable,
then the addition of successive units of capital to the stock
of fixed factors will produce successively smaller increments
of income. This result follows, of course, because the quantity of other factors employed with a unit of capital must
inevitably decrease, as the capital stock increases.

Writers of the "Austrian school" of capital theory employ
a modified version of this case for diminishing returns which
stresses the increasing cost of capital as a cause of diminishing returns. By their argument, not only are capital assets
employed in combination with other resources to create
income, the construction of an additional capital asset
entails the use of existing capital assets and resources.

the economy as a whole, there are diminishing returns to investment if,
and only if, one factor (land in Senior's scheme) is in fixed supply. *An
Outline of the Science of Political Economy* (London, 1836), especially pp. 208–10.

98 Returns to Investment

Hence the additional capital asset created has a cost of production which is the consumption that is sacrificed when other capital assets and resources are diverted to its construction. Part of this sacrifice is temporary; it will end when the new asset is finished and the new asset and resources used in its production are freed for other uses. Part of the sacrifice is permanent, for the new capital asset must be maintained and ultimately replaced. Some capital assets and resources must be assigned to these tasks. Therefore, capital assets are produced under conditions of increasing cost. The addition to (permanent) income which results from the construction of an additional capital asset must decline as the stock of capital assets increases.[4]

The Austrian demonstration that when capital assets have a cost of production there exists diminishing returns to investment is ingenious but quite unnecessary. All that is needed to insure diminishing returns "in the long run" is the presence of a fixed factor of production. Even if the businessman could create capital by waving a wand, wand-waving would be subject to diminishing returns provided that some factor indispensable in production remains in fixed supply.

An exhaustive critique of the case for diminishing returns in the static state would involve us in an unrewarding analysis of the assumptions underlying the static state itself. For our purposes, it will suffice to note that, *a priori*, there is no good reason to posit the peculiar production function that it employs. That is, there is no reason to assume that capital is a variable factor while all other factors are fixed. There is even less reason to assume that while labor and

---

[4] For the original version of the above argument, see E. Böhm-Bawerk, *Capital and Interest*, translated by G. D. Huncke (3 vols.; South Holland, Ill., 1959), II, 102–18.

capital can be employed to create more capital, a similar combination cannot be made to yield more labor. No one doubts that, in the real world, labor skills are created mainly by investment.

One can hardly object to the proposition that, if technology is given, capital accumulation is subject to diminishing returns provided that other factors do not increase proportionately. But here again we have not a theory of diminishing returns relevant to the real world but merely a reworded statement of the law of variable proportions.

The main reasons for believing that the concept of the static state has little to contribute to an understanding of the investment process have been indicated above. There is, however, one version of the static state that is useful because strictly speaking it is not static. In the truly static state, the knowledge of production possibilities is given and the economy has attained long-run equilibrium in the sense that every commodity is already produced in the most efficient manner. Whether in this situation any capital accumulation is possible is a moot point. We can gain some insight into the mechanics of the investment process by retaining the first postulate and dropping the second. That is, we can assume that, as of now, the production of new knowledge suddenly ceases but that the economy has not yet made full use of all knowledge previously discovered. This is analogous to analyzing the flow of water through a distribution system on the assumption that the water supply in the central reservoir has suddenly become "given." For some interval of time, the capital stock will continue to grow as the economy makes use of its hitherto unexploited knowledge of production possibilities.

Viewed in this perspective, the stock of capital assets grows as inferior production techniques give way to im-

proved ones, i.e., as the existing set of capital assets is
employed not to replace itself but to produce a better set.
The rate at which improved techniques replace inferior
techniques depends mainly upon four things: 1) the margin
of superiority of the new method over the old; 2) the flex-
ibility of the existing capital stock, e.g., the cost of shifting
an automobile assembly line to truck manufacture; 3) the
rate at which items in the existing capital stock depreciate;
4) the economy's taste for investment.

Of these factors the first three can be lumped together
under the heading of "the cost of change-over." For two
very good reasons, economists usually assume that this cost
is often "prohibitive" in the short run and minimal in the
long run. In the short run many (if not most) capital assets
are specialized to a narrow range of uses. In the long run
(almost) every capital asset wears out and must be replaced. In the exceptional case of the obsolete asset which
is not part of a "system," e.g., the one-horse shay, it costs
nothing to replace such an asset with a better one. In the
normal case of the obsolete asset which forms part of a
system, e.g., a steam locomotive, there is a cost of changing
over to the better asset. This cost exists because the substitution of the better asset involves the scrapping of some
assets in the system which are not yet fully depreciated.
Properly understood, the phenomenon of "diminishing returns to investment" is an aspect of this cost of change-over.

Let us first consider the impact of innovation on an
industry that makes a negligible—and hence ignorable—
claim on the economy's resources. This postulate of unimportance allows us to assume that the industry's activities
are on too small a scale to affect "the rate of interest"
which, in this context, is another name for the marginal

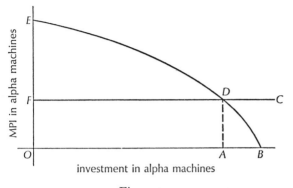

Figure 7.1

productivity of investment (MPI) prevailing in all other industries.

Let us suppose that the industry is initially equipped with a set of alpha machines that wear out at a constant rate—say one a year. The service provided by an alpha machine is subject to the law of diminishing demand. Therefore, the MPI of alpha machines declines as their number increases. This relationship is given in figure 7.1 where the MPI schedule is the curve *EDB*. The industry will build alpha machines until their MPI is equal to the interest rate *OF* (or *AD*)—that is, until "discounted earnings equal cost of production." Figure 7.1 indicates that the industry will invest the sum *OA* in alpha machines, replacing each one as it wears out.

Now suppose that the industry's engineers devise an improved machine, the beta, which is a perfect substitute for existing alpha equipment in the sense that it yields the same type of service. By definition, a given sum invested in beta machines yields a greater return than the same sum invested in alpha machines. Also, by definition, alpha

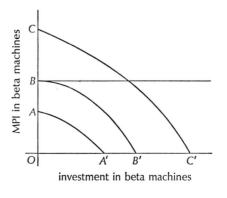

Figure 7.2

machines are obsolete. They may continue in use for a time but no new ones will be built. Clearly the rate of investment in beta machinery depends on its margin of superiority over the older alpha machines, the number of alpha machines in use, and the rate of interest. This dependence is described in figures 7.2 and 7.3. As time passes and alpha machines wear out, the MPI in beta machines increases.

In figure 7.2, curve AA' gives, for different sums that might be invested in beta machines "now," the corresponding MPI. Curve CC' gives, for different investments in beta machines the corresponding MPI "later" when all alpha machines have been retired. In figure 7.2, the rate of interest is a constant OB. No beta machine will be built until MPI rises above OB. Thereafter beta machines will be added at a rate that keeps MPI equal to OB.

The connection between investment in beta machines and depreciation on alpha machines can also be conveyed with the aid of a three dimensional diagram. In figure 7.3 the rate of interest is again a constant; it is represented by the height of plane $WXYZ$. The construction of beta ma-

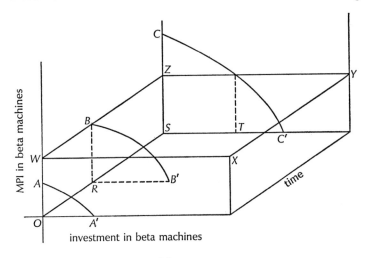

Figure 7.3

chines will not begin immediately after their development;
for curve AA' then nowhere rises above the interest plane.
Investment in beta machines begins after the time interval
OR has elapsed and continues during the time interval RS.
In this last interval, the sum ST is invested in beta machines. Curve CC' in figure 7.3 (as in figure 7.2) is the
MPI schedule for investment in beta machines when the
last alpha machine is fully depreciated.

Figure 7.3 shows both the rate of investment in beta
machines and the sum ultimately to be invested in them.
Note, however, that it does not indicate whether this sum
will be equal to, less than, or more than the maximum
sum formerly invested in alpha machines. To make this
comparison we must have additional information on the
technical superiority of the new machine over the old,
and the demand for the services of these machines. If the
new machine were vastly superior to the old—and if de-

mand for their common product were inelastic—the introduction of the improved model could result in disinvestment in the industry. (The limiting case is the invention so efficient that its service becomes a free good.) Still, if technical progress does not increase investment in the industry where it occurs, it necessarily increases demand for the products of other industries, so that the ultimate result of any invention is growth in the economy's stock of capital assets.

Actually this last result is dictated by our all-inclusive definition of capital taken from Irving Fisher. We have equated capital with "productive power" and so included labor skills. Given this usage, it is meaningless to speak of a "capital saving innovation." One can speak of a machinery saving innovation; but such an innovation merely shifts investment from inanimate things to human beings.

The MPI Schedule for All Capital Assets

It is an easy matter to construct a schedule that shows MPI for a particular type of capital asset. This schedule is the demand curve for assets of this particular type, and since the demand for a capital asset is "derived" from the demand for its services, the meaning of this schedule is clear enough. The construction of a schedule that shows MPI for capital assets "in general" is a more involved undertaking. We note immediately that this aggregate MPI schedule cannot be obtained by summing up the separate MPI schedules for different type capital assets.

In the case of one type of capital asset, the negative slope of the MPI schedule is implied by the negative slope of the demand curve for its services. The price of electricity falls as the quantity supplied increases; therefore, the rate of return on investment in electric generators falls as the number in use increases. But if Say's Law is valid, there exists no negatively inclined demand curve for "services in general" and, hence, none for "capital assets in general."

Nevertheless, economists usually assume that an increase in the capital stock will be accompanied by a fall in MPI provided that the increase is big enough and fast enough. The logic of this position has already been suggested. Capital assets are both specialized and durable. So long as the introduction of new type capital assets is phased in with depreciation on old type capital assets, the capital stock increases without any decline in MPI. Any major effort to accelerate the introduction of new equipment entails the diversion of specialized capital assets from the uses for which they were designed. And the more rapidly the new equipment is introduced, the greater will be the amount of consumption sacrificed relative to the additional capital added. In this sense—and in this sense only—the production of additional capital assets is always subject to diminishing returns.

In fine, although the MPI schedules for the single investment and the capital stock both slope downward, they do so for different reasons. For the single investment, diminishing returns is mainly a demand phenomenon. For the capital stock, it is wholly a supply phenomenon. As time passes, however, the MPI schedules for the single investment and the capital stock shift upward and for the same reason: the continuing depreciation of obsolete type capital assets allows new (improved) types to be introduced without any sacrifice of consumption.

Figure 7.4 does for the capital stock what figure 7.3

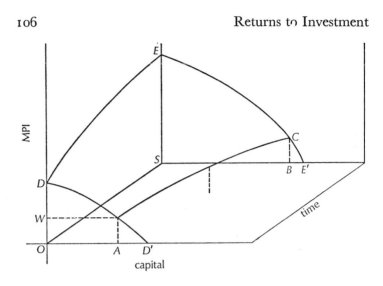

Figure 7.4

does for the single investment. It shows that any increase
in the capital stock will lower MPI, but also that, at any
given moment, invention together with the depreciation
of existing capital assets is a force serving to raise the MPI
schedule.

In the case of the single investment, the rule was inferred that investment in the new type of capital asset
would occur at a rate which kept its MPI equal to the
interest rate (defined as the MPI of the capital stock). No
similar rule can apply to additions to the total capital
stock since its MPI and the rate of interest are the same
thing. We can only infer that the economy will add to its
capital stock at a rate which keeps MPI equal to its marginal rate of substitution of capital assets (investment) for
consumption. In any particular segment of time, capital
accumulation may be accompanied by an increasing, de-

creasing, or constant MPI. The actual behavior of MPI will depend upon the assumptions we make about the effect of an increase in the capital stock on the taste for investment.

Thus figure 7.4 is only a statement of technological possibilities. It does not tell us what the capital stock or MPI is at any point in time—only what it could be. Suppose, for example, that the economy has saved enough in the past to have "now" a capital stock equal to OA and an MPI equal to OW. Figure 7.4 indicates that if, in the time interval OS the economy saves at a rate which keeps MPI equal to OW, then the capital stock will grow to SB. Note that BC equals OW and that in the time interval OS the MPI schedule moves upward from DD' to EE'.

A Note on Lerner's Capital Theory

Since the terminology of capital theory is most confusing, there may be merit in relating the above discussion to A. P. Lerner's treatment of capital accumulation—a treatment that is at once influential, rigorous, and original. Actually, Lerner has offered two versions of capital theory and both deserve careful attention.

Lerner's original version[5] is founded on a distinction between the social marginal productivity of capital and the marginal efficiency of investment which at one point is equated with the private marginal productivity of capital.[6] In this version, capital accumulation occurs whenever the social marginal productivity of capital exceeds the marginal efficiency of investment. Technical progress is identified as

[5] *The Economics of Control* (New York, 1944), pp. 323–45; "Capital, Investment, and Interest," in *Essays in Economic Analysis* (London, 1953), pp. 347–54.
[6] "Capital, Investment, and Interest," p. 350.

the force that tends to keep them apart and investment the force that tends to close the gap.[7]

Our first task is to comprehend the meaning of Lerner's key terms and this is not easy. What we have termed the marginal productivity of investment appears to correspond closely to Lerner's marginal efficiency of investment (MEI). Although he treats MEI and the interest rate as separate variables, MEI in his analysis is always equal to the interest rate. And "for every rate of interest there is a corresponding investment, and the lower the rate of interest the greater the demand for and the output of assets and the greater the rate of investment."[8]

The hard problem is to see what Lerner means by the marginal social productivity of capital (MPC). It does not appear to correspond to the definition of the marginal productivity of capital noted in chapter 4 where the distinction between investment productivity and capital productivity was traced to a gestation period for capital assets. Lerner holds that one must distinguish between MEI and MPC because society, unlike the individual, is not able to obtain assets instantaneously by buying or borrowing.

In order to be able to speak about the marginal productivity of capital from the point of view of the whole economy, economists must compare two stationary economies with a small difference in the quantity of capital equipment but with the same quantity of other factors, land, labor, etc., each stationary economy being perfectly adjusted to a state of affairs that is expected to remain unchanged forever. . . . If this is done it is possible to speak of the difference in the outputs as the marginal product of the increment of capital. If the difficulties arising from the hetero-

---

[7] "Only in a stationary society does this difference disappear, and then the marginal productivity of capital and MEI are both equal to the rate of interest." *The Economics of Control*, p. 335.

[8] *The Economics of Control*, p. 334.

geneity of both capital goods and consumption goods were overcome so that we could express the difference in capital goods of the two economies in terms of a quantity of homogeneous consumption goods, it would be possible to express the marginal productivity of capital as a percentage of so much per annum. When we have done this we must admit that there is no reason for expecting the social marginal productivity of capital to be equal to the interest rate. Only if society, like an individual, could instantaneously increase or decrease its capital by *buying* an increment of capital whenever the yield was greater than the rate of interest, or *selling* it when the yield was less would this equality tend to be brought about.[9]

The above argument is not easy to follow. Lerner rightly cites the necessity of reasoning as if the quantity of capital could be expressed as the equivalent of some quantity of homogeneous consumption goods. This is most easily done by resorting again to the Crusonia model where capital and income can be expressed as so many units of Crusonia. In an economy of Crusonia plants, there would be no meaningful distinction between MEI and MPC. The only relevant technological factor would be the natural growth rate of the plants that establishes MPI and, hence, the rate of interest.

Nor is it economically significant, as Lerner contends, that the individual can "immediately" vary his personal capital stock while society cannot. This difference also characterizes the Crusonia model. The maximum rate at which the economy can add to its capital stock is given by the natural growth rate of its plants. An individual may increase his private holding of Crusonia vegetation by more than this percentage simply by borrowing. The amount of his borrowing, however, cannot cause the rate of interest to diverge from MPI as established by the natural growth

[9] *Ibid.*, p. 332.

rate of the capital stock. For, to repeat, lending at interest
and direct investment are merely two different ways of
increasing income. Nobody borrows at a rate above MPI.
Nobody lends at a rate below MPI. The important dimen-
sion in Lerner's paradox is not *time* but *cost*. And the cost
of adding to the stock of capital assets is the same for the
individual as for the society. In short, there is no paradox.

Nevertheless, it is Lerner's choice of words that is at
fault rather than his insight when he writes: "If the marginal productivity of capital is greater than the rate of
interest, net investment will be positive and the capital
equipment will be increasing." Or again: "Investment will
be carried on at that rate per unit of time which makes
MEI equal the rate of interest "[10] To make the first proposition correct, it is only necessary to define MPC as what MEI
will be when all obsolete capital assets have been scrapped.
(This definition supposes that no new inventions are made
in this time interval.) Lerner's second proposition need
only be altered to read: Investment will be carried on at
that rate per unit of time which makes MEI equal to the
marginal rate of substitution of consumption for capital
assets.

In a subsequent article, Lerner argued that the distinction between the marginal social productivity of capital
and the marginal efficiency of investment was meaningless
and should be discarded.[11] This recommendation is based
upon the recognition that "in general there can never be
any clear meaning in the comparison of the marginal
product of capital with the rate of interest." It is pointless

[10] *Ibid.*, p. 335.
[11] "On the Marginal Product of Capital and the Marginal Efficiency of
Investment," *Journal of Political Economy*, LXI (1953), 1-14.

to attempt a comparison because "all the problems that look like capital problems turn out to be investment problems."[12] One is left then with the schedule that gives the marginal efficiency of investment So far, so good.

At this point, however, Lerner erroneously argues that the effect of investment is to lower this schedule,[13] whereas, in fact, investment only moves the economy to a lower point on the curve. The MEI schedule, in a world of perfect certainty, could only fall if some part of the economy's knowledge of production possibilities were somehow destroyed. In the normal course of events, knowledge always increases and the MEI schedule is constantly pushed upward. In ridding his system of the marginal social productivity of capital, Lerner would seem to have assumed away technical progress—the phenomenon whose effect on the rate of interest it helped to clarify.

A Concluding Caution

Our discussion of the forces that determine MPI in the real world can profitably end with the recognition of a major pitfall in theorizing about capital accumulation. The pitfall awaits anyone who treats MPI solely as a function of the size of the capital stock and so is led to conclude that capital accumulation is characterized by diminishing returns in the long run as well as in the short run. Properly viewed, MPI is also, at any given moment, a function of the technical superiority of new machines over old, the number of old machines in existence, the age composition of these old machines, and the rate at which they depreci-

[12] *Ibid.*, p. 8.
[13] *Ibid.*, pp. 9–10.

ate. In the interest of simplifying the analysis, this chapter
has lumped these other factors under the heading of "time"
and assumed that the passage of time always serves to raise
the MPI schedule.

CHAPTER 8

Production with a

Fixed Factor

So far we have held fast to the proposition that capital is
the only factor of production and, by implication, that
anything useful in production is capital. From this tenacity,
it follows that it is meaningless to speak of the marginal
product of capital; there are no other factors to which capital
can be added or from which it can be subtracted. In the
normal case of constant capital accumulation, capital is
added to itself by investment in order to increase income.
The economically significant datum is the cost of the additional income obtained as measured by amount of consumption sacrificed to obtain it.

When capital and income are a homogeneous, consumable substance, and there is no period of production, one
can speak of the marginal productivity of investment in
capital assets (there being nothing else in which to invest).
As we have seen, when income Y is solely a function of
capital K, this marginal productivity is $\frac{dY}{dK}$.

In a world of continuous innovation, income is also a
function of the point in time at which production occurs.
In this chapter, however, our concern is with the complications introduced into capital theory by the postulate that
production is carried on with two factors, one fixed and
the other variable. Therefore, there is no point in treating
Y as a function of time. Now $Y = f(K, L_0)$ where L_0 (for
land) denotes the fixed factor. Since the supply of land is

unalterable, the marginal productivity of investment is the partial derivative, $\dfrac{\partial Y}{\partial K}$.

Chapter 2 argued that the main justification for treating capital as the only factor of production is that, in the real world, most of the things useful in production are created by investment and destroyed by use, so that, given enough time, one set of specialized men and machines can be used to create a different set of specialized men and machines. Nevertheless, the practice of treating capital as but one of several factors of production is of long standing in economic analysis. The false view that land is in fixed supply is especially resistant to eradication. Moreover, since the creation and destruction of certain specialized capital assets can be exceedingly costly in the short run if attempted on a large scale, it is sometimes useful to reason "as if" they constitute a fixed factor. For these reasons, in this chapter we shall consider the case of production with two factors, one fixed and the other variable.

The Generality of the Two Factor Case

In capital theory scarcely any good purpose is served by positing more than two factors of production. All things useful in production that can be created by investment and destroyed by use are capital, i.e., stored-up consumption, and hence the same thing. If the production function contains two such variable factors, then their marginal productivities will, of course, be equal in equilibrium. For if at any moment they are not equal, the factor with the lower marginal productivity will be consumed and the factor with the higher marginal productivity will be increased by investment. This process of adjustment in factor supplies will continue until either the two marginal productivities are equal or the "inferior" factor has been wholly consumed.

All things useful in production that cannot be created by investment and destroyed by use are not capital (or stored-up consumption). As these things are axiomatically in fixed supply, except as this supply is increased by some unidentified force in the universe, it does not matter what they are "intrinsically." A fixed factor has value to the extent that it is useful in production and scarce relative to the variable factor. The process by which the fixed factor is valued is of some interest in capital theory mainly because it looms so large in the history of economic doctrine. We shall consider this particular problem of imputation, albeit briefly. This perfunctory treatment is justified because, on close examination, it will turn out to be a special case of the diminishing returns to investment problem discussed in chapter 4.

In chapter 4, diminishing returns were obtained by making income Y solely a function of capital K and assuming that any part of the capital stock ceased to grow when cut away from the parent plant preparatory to consumption. Recall that this last assumption was necessary because, without it, the economy would divide the capital stock whenever diminishing returns threatened and so escape them. In this chapter, a different assumption is employed to insure diminishing returns to investment. We secure this result by positing a fixed factor.

The Adding-Up Problem Reopened

When production is carried on with two factors, one fixed and the other variable, the task facing economists is to discern the principle or principles that govern the distribution of income. This is the venerable "adding-up"

problem of economic theory. The main outlines of the
answer were sketched many years ago, notably by J. B.
Clark and Philip Wicksteed.[1] Economists, however, have a
predilection for discussing this problem on the assumption
that the production function is homogeneous and of the
first degree.[2] This bias is both understandable and defensi-
ble. It dictates that there are constant returns to scale—
that output can always be doubled by doubling the amount
of each factor used. And since this assumption is as reasonable as any other, there is usually little to be gained by
foregoing the simplifications it makes possible. Nevertheless, the popularity of the production function that is
homogeneous and of the first degree has probably delayed
the exposition of the complete solution to the adding-up
problem. It may also have obscured the role of the interest
rate and the capitalization process in affording a specious
validity to what is commonly called the "marginal productivity theory of distribution."[3]

Let us return to first principles and consider how output

[1] Clark, *The Distribution of Wealth* (New York, 1899), pp. 173–76, 200–5;
Wicksteed, *Co-ordination of the Laws of Distribution* (London, 1894).

[2] An equation is homogeneous if the sums of the exponents of the variables
in all terms are equal. An equation is of the first degree if the sum of the
exponents in every term is unity.

[3] The popularity of the production function that is homogeneous and of
the first degree ("linear") also developed because economists undertook to
solve the adding-up problem while they were still struggling, in the pre-
Fisher era, to lay the foundations of capital theory. The use of this function
allowed them to "exhaust the product" without having any clear view of
the relations among the average productivity of investment, the marginal
productivity of investment (the rate of interest), capital, and income.
These remarks apply with particular force to Wicksell who consciously
sought to integrate capital theory and distribution theory. His efforts
must be counted a gallant failure since he mistook the rate of interest for
the average productivity of investment and defined capital as saved-up
labor and land. Yet since Wicksell knew about linear production functions,
his treatment of distribution is wholly "modern." *Lectures on Political Economy*,
translated from the Swedish by E. Classen (2 vols.; London, 1934), especially Vol. I, Part II.

is divided in three different situations. Throughout the following discussion we shall assume that production is carried on with the variable factor, capital, and the fixed factor, "land"; and that the suppliers of these factors are numerous enough to insure perfect competition on the supply side of the factors market. We shall not in every case assume perfect competition on the demand side of the factors market. The reason for this inconsistency will emerge in the discussion.

Consider all production functions whose descriptive equations are given by

$$Y = a(KL_0)^{1/n} \qquad (1)$$

where Y = income
$\quad K$ = capital
$\quad L_0$ = a fixed quantity of "land"
$\quad a > 0$
$\quad n \geq 1$

Distribution with Constant Returns to Scale

The case of constant returns to scale prevails when, in equation (1), $n = 2$. Here, when each factor receives its marginal physical product, "payments to the factors exactly exhaust the product," i.e., $\frac{\partial Y}{\partial K} K + \frac{\partial Y}{\partial L} L = Y$. This is the easy part of the adding-up problem. A simple geometrical solution is given in figure 8.1.

For a constant quantity of land $L = L_0$, and a momentary stock of capital OA, we can read off the following information from this figure:

$$AB = OD = \text{income}$$

$$\frac{AB}{FA} = \frac{DE}{DB} = \text{the rate of interest}$$

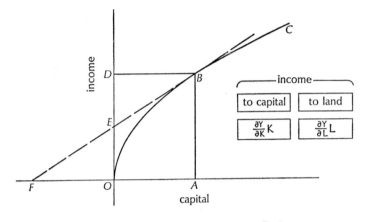

Figure 8.1: Constant Returns to Scale

DE = capital's share of income

EO = land's share of income

$\dfrac{EO}{L_0}$ = rent per unit of land

Figure 8.1 provides no direct information on the marginal productivity of land, $\dfrac{\partial Y}{\partial L}$. But since $Y = a(LK)^{1/2}$, $Y - \dfrac{\partial Y}{\partial K} K = \dfrac{\partial Y}{\partial L} L$. It follows that EO is the surplus remaining after DE has been paid to capital. Assuming that each unit of land is paid the same, $\dfrac{\partial Y}{\partial L} = \dfrac{EO}{L_0}$.

Distribution with Increasing Returns to Scale

The case of increasing returns to scale prevails when, in equation (1), $1 \leq n < 2$. Here, when each factor receives its marginal physical product, "payments to the factors exceed the product," i.e., $\frac{\partial Y}{\partial K} K + \frac{\partial Y}{\partial L} L > Y$.

Now two things are obvious. Payment according to marginal physical productivity is an economic impossibility. If one factor receives its marginal physical product, the other does not. The efficient organization of production requires that there be only one firm, i.e., "monopoly."

Given increasing returns to scale, what principle does, in fact, govern the distribution of the product? In the two-factor case of equation (1), three possible answers can readily be discerned.

1. The variable factor, capital, is paid its marginal physical product; the fixed factor, land, receives the surplus.

2. The fixed factor, land, is paid its marginal physical product; the variable factor, capital, receives the surplus.

3. The division of the product is determined by the relative marginal physical productivities of the factors.[4] That is, if G_K denotes the payment per unit of capital and G_L denotes the payment per unit of land, then the equilibrium values for G_K and G_L are obtained by solving

$$KG_K + LG_L = Y$$

$$\frac{G_K}{G_L} = \frac{\dfrac{\partial Y}{\partial K}}{\dfrac{\partial Y}{\partial L}} \tag{2}$$

[4] Distribution according to relative marginal productivity seems to be Professor Allais' theory of factor shares. "By definition the primary income is imputed proportionally to the marginal productivities in physical values." "The Influence of the Capital-Output Ratio on Real National Income," *Econometrica,* XXX (1962), 705.

A moment's reflection will show that the first answer is the correct one. The variable factor, capital, is paid its marginal physical product; the fixed factor, land, receives the surplus. Here the important and decisive truth is that capital and land are compensated according to different principles simply because the supply of capital is variable while the supply of land is fixed.[5]

Capital can be created by not consuming income and destroyed by consuming at a rate greater than income. We assume that, in the case of every investor, the higher the rate of interest, the greater the quantity of capital assets that he is prepared to hold, i.e., the greater the fraction of income that he is prepared to invest. Therefore, any cut in the remuneration of investors ("capitalists") will cause them to hold a smaller quantity of capital assets than otherwise. Any fall in the capital stock will reduce income, the total rent bill, and rent per acre. The inability of landlords to secure the marginal physical product of land will produce no such result since, axiomatically, land cannot be "consumed."

The division of the product in the case of increasing returns to scale is described in figure 8.2. When the capital stock is OA, marginal productivity of investment is $\frac{BA}{FA}$ (or DE/DB); and capital's share is DE. The surplus EO is paid for the use of land and payment per unit of land is EO/L_0.

The necessity of the above result—that capital shall be

[5] Note, however, that the argument that, under increasing returns to scale, factors are paid according to relative marginal productivity is relevant to the three factor case. When production is carried on with capital and two fixed factors, capital will receive its marginal physical product and the surplus will be divided between the fixed factors according to their relative marginal productivities.

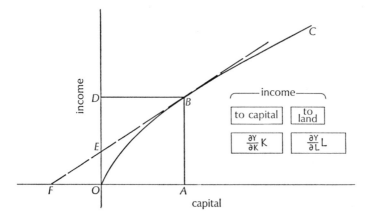

Figure 8.2: Increasing Returns to Scale

paid its marginal physical product with the surplus going to land—can perhaps be more easily seen with the aid of the following example. Suppose that, at the beginning of each year, would-be entrepreneurs bid for the right to organize production. Suppose that the bidding is subject to the following restrictions: 1) All bids must be "realistic" in that they cannot promise more product to the factors than will be produced; 2) All would-be entrepreneurs must bid simultaneously for specified quantities of capital and land; 3) A bid, to be successful, must be accepted by both capitalists and landlords; 4) The bidding cannot stop until all the proffered capital and land has been contracted for. (We assume that "entrepreneurship" is not a scarce factor of production and hence receives no part of the product.)

Given increasing returns to scale, all bids will be preemptive in the first round. Parties to the bidding will offer the whole of the product to capitalists and landlords; the greatest total factor payment can be offered by him who seeks to hire all of the available factors. Our problem is to demonstrate that, on the rules laid down above, the only bid which is final is that which gives capital its marginal physical product.

Consider what would happen if two different preemptive bids were submitted in the first round of bidding. The first bid gives capital its marginal physical product; the second gives capital more than its marginal physical product and so leaves less product to be divided among landlords. Clearly capitalists will wish to accept the second offer while landlords will prefer the first. Thus it will be necessary to bid again.

In the second round of bidding, it will be possible for someone to better the second of the original preemptive bids—that which promised capital more than its marginal physical product. This can be done by submitting a bid which is not preemptive in that it offers to hire all available land, but offers to hire a little less than the whole of available capital. Such a bid contemplates a reduction of the ratio of capital to land in the factor combination, hence it can match the highest of the previous bids for capital and offer a higher rent for land.

However, this less-than-preemptive bid of the second round cannot "dominate" a preemptive bid which promises capital its marginal physical product and the surplus to land. For landlords will still prefer this latter preemptive bid and another round of bidding is in order. The process will continue until all bids which promise capital more than its marginal physical product have been screened out.

Note that our conclusion that land will collect the surplus depends on the assumption that the "monopolist" (whoever or whatever he is) enjoys no legal protection; he must bid in a purely competitive market for the right to organize production. If the monopolist enjoyed complete legal protection, he would, of course, be able to appropriate the whole of the landlords' share and some part of the capitalists' share. Since the supply of capital is not fixed but depends upon the willingness of capitalists to refrain from consumption, the monopolist will find it to his interest to pay something for the use of capital in order to obtain the quantity that will maximize his profit.

Spurious Distribution According to Marginal Productivity

Probably it would be better if economists did not speak of the "marginal product" of a fixed factor used in combination with a variable factor. The total value of land in terms of income can be obtained by discounting its share of income by the rate of interest. This discount rate is, in turn, equal to the marginal productivity of investment in the variable factor, i.e., equal to $\frac{\partial Y}{\partial K}$. When the discount operation is performed in figure 8.2, the value of land is seen to be FO. Given $L = L_0$, the rent per unit of land is EO/L_0. It follows that if "investment in land" is defined not as L_0 but rather as FO, and the unit rental is EO/L_0, then investment in land gives the return EO/FO and "payments to the factors exhaust the product." This result is trivial. It merely shows that given a market in which claims to income are traded and a positive rate of interest, the present value of a future income is obtained by discounting it.[6]

[6] For modern expositions of distribution theory that exhaust the product with a nonlinear production function by capitalizing the shares of fixed factors, see J. M. Henderson and R. E. Quandt, *Microeconomic Theory: A Mathematical Approach* (New York, 1958), pp. 64–65; and H. H. Liebhafsky, *The Nature of Price Theory* (Homewood, 1963), pp. 317–18.

Distribution with Decreasing Returns to Scale

The case of decreasing returns to scale prevails when, in equation (1), $n > 2$. Here, when each factor receives its marginal product, the sum of the payments to the factors is less than output, i.e., $\frac{\partial Y}{\partial K} K + \frac{\partial Y}{\partial L} L < Y$. Admittedly it is impossible to have decreasing returns to scale for all values of K and L. For on this (economically) impossible assumption, there is no limit to the amount of output (Y) obtainable from any given quantity of capital and land. One could always increase output by dividing the factor amounts among a greater number of firms, so that an infinitely large output could be obtained by using an infinite number of infinitely small firms. For this reason, economists have often dismissed the case of decreasing returns to scale as unworthy of study.

Nevertheless, the case of decreasing returns to scale can be made economically meaningful by a minor change in our assumptions. We need only posit that there is a limit to the number of parts into which the fixed factor can be divided. On this assumption we may construct figure 8.3. If the fixed factor can be divided into m parts, then efficient production requires that resources be allocated equally among m firms. Curve OC is drawn on the assumption that, whatever the size of the capital stock, resources are so allocated. Thus when the capital stock is OA, each firm uses OA/m capital and L_0/m land. Once again the marginal productivity of capital is given by AB/FA (or DE/DB), and capital's share of income is given by DE. But given decreasing returns to scale and a maximum number of firms, landlords will receive less than EO.

What is the nature of the undistributed surplus that re-

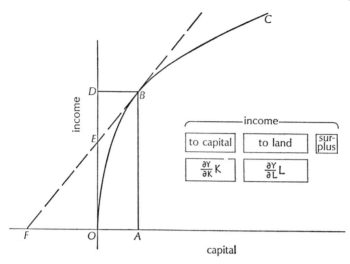

Figure 8.3: Decreasing Returns to Scale

mains after capital and land have been paid their marginal product? It can be accurately, if inelegantly, described as payment for entrepreneurial living space. The surplus is, in fact, analogous to the rent of location inevitably earned by a television station because the need for clear reception imposes a limit on the number of stations that can be allowed to transmit. If the rights to a share of this surplus are freely transferable, they will be capitalized at the rate of interest established by the marginal productivity of investment in capital. Capital, by definition, is the only thing in which the economy can invest.

Ought we to regard "entrepreneurial living space" as a third hidden factor of production? This is an issue of semantics and can be left to individual taste. Since factor divisibility is not usually regarded as a separate factor of production, my own prejudice is that the part of the product remaining after capital and land have received their marginal physical products can unashamedly be treated as a surplus.

A Perspective on the "Ricardo Effect"

The geometry of this chapter can be used to clarify a long-standing dispute among economists on the effect of an increase in the real wage on the ratio of capital to labor in the factor combination. At most times and places, most economists have accepted Ricardo's proposition that a rise in the real wage will cause employers to substitute machinery for labor in the factor combination. "Machinery and labour are in constant competition, and the former can frequently not be employed until labour rises."[7] A few economists, however, have demurred. They have done so mainly on the ground that, inasmuch as machinery is made with labor, a rise in the cost of labor is also a rise in the cost of machinery, so that employers have no incentive to substitute machinery for labor unless the wage increase is accompanied by a fall in the rate of interest which cuts the cost of machinery.[8]

Figure 8.1 suggests that there is something to be said for both views, but, also, that their exponents employ different assumptions. Assume that the future is certain, factor markets are purely competitive, and labor (rather than land) is the fixed factor. Given these postulates, an increase in the capital stock will simultaneously produce both a rise in the real wage and a fall in the rate of interest, i.e., the marginal productivity of investment. Therefore,

---

[7] *On the Principles of Political Economy and Taxation* (3d ed.; London, 1821), p. 479.
[8] See, for example, the review of Hicks on Wages by G. F. Shove, *Economic Journal*, XLIII (1933), 469-72.

it is misleading to describe the increase in the real wage as the "cause" of the increase in capital stock.

Should the real wage rate be raised suddenly above its competitive level by government edict or labor union action, the curve *OC* is lowered in figure 8.1. It can be raised somewhat, though not back to its initial level, by firing some workers and shortening the work week. To the extent that competition in the factor market is not perfect, the effect of increase in the real wage upon the capital-labor ratio depends upon the types of imperfections specified. And here the possibilities are legion. To the extent that labor is not a fixed factor but created by investing consumption, it is not profitable to enquire how the capital-labor ratio is affected by a rise in the real wage. For now the relevant datum is not the real wage itself but the marginal rate of return on investment in labor skills as against the comparable yield on other forms of investment.

Recapitulation

It is sometimes useful to study production on the assumption that it is carried on with two factors, one fixed, the other variable. When this is done, the division of the product is dictated by the type of production posited. The three main types of production functions imply, in turn, constant, increasing, and decreasing returns to scale. The division of the product and the equilibrium number of firms corresponding to these possibilities are summarized in table 8.1. We note that in all three cases the variable factor, capital, is paid its marginal physical product.

We are now able to form a clearer view of verbal ambiguities that encrust many expositions of the so-called marginal productivity theory of distribution. Consider the familiar statement that given perfect competition in factor

TABLE 8.1. Equilibrium Product Division:
Two Factor Case

Returns to scale	Capital's share	Land's share	Surplus	Number of firms
constant	$\dfrac{\partial Y}{\partial K} K$	$\dfrac{\partial Y}{\partial L} L$	0	indeterminate
increasing	$\dfrac{\partial Y}{\partial K} K$	$Y - \dfrac{\partial Y}{\partial K} K$	0	1
decreasing	$\dfrac{\partial Y}{\partial K} K$	$\dfrac{\partial Y}{\partial L} L$	> 0	constant*

* The number of firms is equal to the number of parts into which the fixed factor, land, can be divided.

and product markets, in equilibrium each factor will be paid its marginal product and payments to the factors will exactly exhaust the product.

If the "quantity" of a factor is viewed as a certain quantity of *exchange* value, the statement is true but trivial. Anything or anybody that collects a part of the product is by definition a factor of production. Given a rate of interest, all shares of the product will be capitalized and all "investments" will earn the same rate of return.

If the quantity of a factor is viewed as some physical quantity—man-hours, acres, tons, etc.—the foregoing statement is maddeningly ambiguous since nothing is said about returns to scale. If constant returns to scale are assumed, the statement is redundant. A small firm is as efficient as a giant, entry into the business of combining factors is free, there is no way entrepreneurs can avoid paying each factor its marginal physical product (free entry ensuring this result), and it is an algebraic necessity that payments to the factors exhaust the product. Strictly speaking, perfect competition *is* the case where production is carried on with constant returns to scale.

If constant returns to scale are not assumed, the statement under discussion is highly misleading. Increasing returns to scale insure monopoly, but, while payments to the factors exhaust the product, the fixed factor receives less than its marginal physical product. Decreasing returns to scale (with some limit to the divisibility of the fixed factor) is compatible with any finite number of firms and hence with the semblance of "perfect competition." But now, while each factor receives its marginal physical product, payments to the factors do not exhaust the product.

We might conclude by asking if there is any reason to perpetuate the division in economics between capital theory and distribution theory. For the important verity is that capital—the stock of all things which can be created by investment and destroyed by use—will receive its marginal physical product irrespective of the type of production function assumed. All things useful in production which cannot be so created and destroyed will receive the surplus that remains after capital has been paid its marginal physical product. The many nineteenth-century economists who were reluctant to discard the concept of a "rent" element in national income—an element that was not distributed according to marginal physical productivity— had a better case than they are given credit for.[9]

[9] Marshall, for example, never did discard his treatment of land rent as a surplus not distributed according to marginal physical productivity. See *Principles of Economics*, (8th ed.; London, 1920), pp. 155–56.

CHAPTER 9   Capital, Technology, and Economic Growth

In recent years, the domain of capital theory has been expanded to include a number of interesting "growth models." [1] In a literal sense, every model of economic activity which allows for the possibility of investment and disinvestment has a claim to this label. For when the marginal productivity of investment (MPI) is greater than zero, income growth is a technical possibility. In the special case where MPI is zero, negative income growth is still a technical possibility; that is, income can be reduced by consuming some part of the capital stock. In the recent literature of economics, however, a "growth model" has acquired an additional and distinctive attribute. It incorporates the possibility that, given enough time, income can increase without any fall in MPI. It implies that there are no diminishing returns to investment provided that the growth rate of the capital stock is low enough.

A Basic Growth Model

As long as technical progress occurs and/or the supply of every factor of production is increasing, there is no reason

[1] See, for example, E. D. Domar, *Essays in the Theory of Economic Growth* (New York, 1957); J. E. Meade, *A Neo-Classical Theory of Economic Growth* (London, 1961); R. M. Solow, "Investment and Technical Progress," in *Mathematical Methods in the Social Sciences*, K. J. Arrow, ed. (Stanford, 1960), pp. 89–104; E. S. Phelps, "Substitution, Fixed Proportions, Growth and Distribution," *International Economic Review*, IV (1963), 265–88; and R. M. Solow, *Capital Theory and the Rate of Return* (Amsterdam, 1963).

capital accumulation should be associated with a falling MPI. Thus there is no reason capital accumulation should ever cease. What then is the meaning of "equilibrium" in a growth model? Let us first consider this question with the aid of a production function that combines two factors of production, capital and labor. Let us also assume (though, after the condemnation of the "static state" in chapter 3, it goes against the grain to do so) that "knowledge" or "the state of technology" is given. On this assumption we have a growth model only because the supply of each factor can be increased over time. The size of the capital stock can be increased by investing (saving) income. The supply of labor is constantly being increased by some unidentified force in the universe. Once more we have recourse to a production function that is linear and homogeneous:

$$Y = K^{1/2}N^{1/2} \tag{1}$$

where Y = income

K = capital

N = labor

$$Y = \frac{\partial Y}{\partial K} K + \frac{\partial Y}{\partial N} N$$

Given equation (1), the increase in income Y is a function of the increase in capital K and the increase in labor N. Thus

$$\Delta Y = (K + \Delta K)^{1/2}(N + \Delta N)^{1/2} - K^{1/2}N^{1/2} \tag{2}$$

or

$$\Delta Y \approx \frac{K^{1/2}}{2N^{1/2}} \Delta N + \frac{N^{1/2}}{2K^{1/2}} \Delta K \tag{2a}$$

The percentage increase in income $\frac{\Delta Y}{Y}$ is

$$\frac{\Delta Y}{Y} \approx \frac{\Delta N}{2N} + \frac{\Delta K}{2K} \tag{3}$$

For brevity we can let y, k, and n denote the percentage changes in Y, K, and N. Equation (3) now becomes

$$y \approx \tfrac{1}{2}k + \tfrac{1}{2}n \tag{3a}$$

If we define "equilibrium" as the case where income grows at a uniform geometric rate—as the case where y is constant—then the capital stock and the labor supply must, in equilibrium, increase at the same rate. By definition, equilibrium has been achieved where $k = n$. This definition of equilibrium is not wholly arbitrary. For if the savings habits of the population are given, any gap between k and n is self-closing. If the capital stock grows more rapidly than the labor supply, MPI $\left(\text{which is } \dfrac{\partial Y}{\partial K}\right)$ will fall. With it will fall the rate of income growth made possible by a given fraction of income saved. If the capital stock grows more slowly than the labor supply, MPI will rise. With it will rise the rate of income growth made possible by a given fraction of income saved. Income growth is "steady" only when the capital stock and the labor supply increase by the same percentage each year.

Note that in our simple growth model there is no unique value for K that is associated with equilibrium defined as the case where income grows at a uniform geometric rate. In fact, in equilibrium the value of K is a function of the fraction of income that the economy chooses to save. The greater the fraction of income saved, the greater the size of the capital stock needed in order to insure that $k = n$. This relationship between the capital stock and the fraction of income saved is dictated by the linearity of the production function. Given equation (1), $\frac{\partial^2 Y}{\partial K^2} < 0$, so that the "efficiency" of savings declines as the ratio of capital to labor increases. But when the object is to maintain a given rate of income growth, the decline in the efficiency of saving resulting from an increase is the ratio of capital to labor can be compensated for (up to a point) by increasing the fraction of income saved.

The nature of equilibrium in a growth model can perhaps be more strikingly conveyed if we assign numerical values to Y, K, N, and n in equation (1). Assume that, as of this moment, $N = 100$ and $n = 0.25$. Table 9.1 gives a sample of the combinations of capital stock K and savings propensity S that are compatible with steady income growth. Table 9.1 also shows for these equilibrium combinations of K and S the following magnitudes that they imply: the marginal productivity of investment $\frac{\partial Y}{\partial K}$, the capital-output ratio Y/K, income invested SY, and income consumed C.

We note the following properties of our growth model.

1. In Table 9.1 every set of values for K, Y, S, SY, C, $\frac{Y}{K}$, and $\frac{\partial Y}{\partial K}$ is compatible with a constant rate of increase in income. Specifically, every set of values for these variables yields $k = n = 0.25$.

2. When $N = 100$ and $n = 0.25$, the equilibrium capital stock cannot exceed 1600 units. For when $K = 1600$, it is possible to have $y = k = n = 0.25$ only if all income is saved. Thus when $K = 1600$, $Y = 400$ and then $Y/K = y = k = n = 0.25$. But if, when $N = 100$ and $n = 0.25$, more than 1600 units of capital were used, the capital-output ratio Y/K would fall below 0.25. It would then be

TABLE 9.1. Possible Equilibriums in a Growth Model

Given: (a) $Y = K^{1/2}N^{1/2}$, (b) $N = 100$, (c) $n = 0.25$

K	0.0016	... 250.	300.	350.	400.	450.	500.	550.	600.	... 1600.
Y	0.4	158.1	173.2	187.1	200.	212.13	223.6	234.5	244.9	400.
S	0.001	0.395	0.433	0.468	0.5	0.53	0.559	0.586	0.612	1.
SY	0.0004	62.45	75.0	87.50	100.	112.50	125.	137.4	149.9	400.
C	0.3996	95.7	98.2	99.54	100.	99.6	98.6	97.1	95.1	0
$\dfrac{Y}{K}$	250.00	0.63	0.57	0.53	0.50	0.47	0.45	0.43	0.41	0.25
$\dfrac{\partial Y}{\partial K}$	125.000	0.316	0.289	0.267	0.25	0.236	0.224	0.213	0.204	0.125

K = capital
Y = income
S = fraction of income saved

SY = income saved
C = income consumed
$\dfrac{Y}{K}$ = capital-output ratio
$\dfrac{\partial Y}{\partial K}$ = marginal productivity of investment (rate of interest)

N = labor
n = growth rate of labor force

impossible to maintain an income growth rate of 0.25 even though the whole of income were saved.

3. A constant rate of income growth is not possible unless some fraction of income is saved. For if $S = 0$ when $n = 0.25$, then $k = SY/K = 0$ and $n > k$.

4. In equilibrium, the rate of income growth is independent of the fraction of income saved. In fact, the equilibrium rate of income growth is the rate n at which the labor supply increases.

5. Nevertheless, by moving from equilibrium to disequilibrium the rate of income growth can temporarily be increased by raising the fraction of income saved (except, of course, in the case where all income is already being saved).

Suppose, for example, the economy is currently in equilibrium with

$$S = 0.433$$
$$K = 300$$
$$Y = 173.2$$
$$SY = 75$$
$$y = k = n = 0.25$$

Now let a sudden increase in the taste for thrift throw the economy into disequilibrium with $S = 0.612$. Given this shock,

$$SY = 106$$
$$\frac{SY}{K} = k = 0.353$$

and, since $y = \frac{1}{2}k + \frac{1}{2}n$,

$$y = 0.302$$

But, because $k > n$, the marginal productivity of investment is falling and will continue to fall until once more

$k = n$. Note that the new equilibrium cannot be shown in table 9.1 since it will be reached with $n = 0.25$ but $N > 100$.

6. The equilibrium level of income Y is a function of the fraction of income saved. The higher this fraction, the higher the equilibrium level of income. Thus, if all income is saved, $S = 1$ and $Y = 400$. If one-half of income is saved, $S = 0.5$ and $Y = 200$.

7. The equilibrium level of consumption C is also a function of the fraction of income saved. But while saving always increases income (as long as MPI is greater than zero), saving does not always increase consumption. The maximum amount of consumption consistent with the steady income growth rate of 0.25 is 100. This level of consumption is achieved when $S = 0.5$. If $S < 0.5$, then both income and consumption are smaller. If $S > 0.5$, income is greater but consumption is smaller.

8. In equilibrium, consumption is greatest when MPI is equal to the growth rate of the capital stock, and hence to the growth rate of the labor supply. The necessity of this equality can be demonstrated as follows given the equilibrium condition that $k = n$.

Since
$$\frac{SY}{K} = k$$

in equilibrium
$$\frac{SY}{K} = n \qquad (4)$$

and
$$S = \frac{nK}{Y} \qquad (4a)$$

Then
$$C = Y - SY \qquad (5)$$

or
$$C = K^{1/2}N^{1/2} - nK \qquad (5a)$$

When
$$\frac{\partial C}{\partial K} = 0$$

then
$$\frac{N^{1/2}}{2K^{1/2}} = n$$

But from equation (1),

$$\frac{\partial Y}{\partial K} = \frac{N^{1/2}}{2K^{1/2}}$$

Consequently, $N^{1/2}/2K^{1/2}$ *is* the marginal productivity of investment.

The rule that, in equilibrium, consumption is greatest when the growth rate of the capital stock is equal to MPI is sometimes given a more arresting formulation. It is said that consumption is greatest when all profits are invested and all wages consumed. This proposition is valid provided that "profits" denote all payments for the use of capital, $\frac{\partial Y}{\partial K} K$, and "wages" denote all payments for the use of labor, $\frac{\partial Y}{\partial N} N$. In table 9.1 consumption is greatest when payments for the use of capital and income invested both equal 100. It is, of course, quite immaterial whether investment sums are supplied by workers, capitalists, or worker-capitalists.[2] It would be much better to say simply: in equilibrium, consumption is greatest when the amount of income invested is equal to the amount of income paid for the use of capital.

Reflecting upon the above matter, some economists have come to consider it a serious indictment of the American economy that the rate of return on capital (as defined by

[2] Joan Robinson, *Essays in the Theory of Economic Growth* (London, 1963), pp. 135–36.

statisticians) is almost invariably above the economy's rate of income growth, and the discrepancy is variously attributed to an excessive propensity to save produced by an unequal distribution of personal income, the imperfections of the capital market, and a foolish underestimation of the pleasures of future consumption. This view of investment implies, of course, that, if consumption per head is to be maximized, the State must intervene to close the gap between investment return and growth rate. No doubt there are many good reasons for arguing that consumption in the United States should grow at a more rapid rate. But it is difficult to give weight to an argument that rests upon a view of the world which categorically divides all productive power into "capital" and "labor."

9. Finally, table 9.1 shows that MPI behaves "normally." That is, the greater the ratio of capital to labor, the lower MPI. Nevertheless, in equilibrium, MPI cannot be less than 0.125. A lower MPI would imply $K > 1600$. But if $K > 1600$, the capital growth rate k would be less than the labor growth rate n even though all income were saved. However, there is no maximum MPI in the model described by table 9.1. For as long as $K < 1600$, there is some fraction of income saved that will yield $k = n$.

Technology and the Production Function

In this chapter and the preceding one we have employed a production function that combines capital with something else. The something else was first land and later labor. When the supply of this something else is fixed, "equilibrium" signifies a constant capital stock, a constant rate of income flow, and no income growth at all. When the supply of this something else grows at some uniform rate, "equi-

librium" signifies that the capital stock and income flow
are increasing at this same rate.

We could, of course, make use of a production function
that combines three or more factors in order to build a
growth model. But the effort would be tedious and the
results uninteresting. We could also drop the assumption
that the growth rate of the second factor—the something
else in the production function—is determined by some
mysterious force. For example, we could make the growth
rate of the labor supply depend upon the fraction of income
saved. Since the size of the human population is clearly
influenced by the "quantity of the means of subsistence"
this step might seem to be justified in the interest of greater
realism. The difficulty with taking this step is that it would
permit "labor" to be created by investing income and so
blur the distinction between capital and labor in the production function. If, in the interest of realism, one specifies
that the growth rate of the labor supply is a function of the
fraction of income saved, one might as well go all the way.
The ultimate realism in capital theory is the recognition of
the truth that no satisfactory distinction can be made between capital and other factors of production.

Many economists who have seriously examined assumptions underlying the production function that combines capital with something else are not especially happy with it,[3]
and their dissatisfaction can be traced, in large part, to its
limitations for dealing with the phenomenon of technical
progress. This phenomenon, in turn, is inseparably bound

[3] See, for example, Joan Robinson, "The Production Function and the
Theory of Capital," *Review of Economic Studies*, XXI (1953–54), 81–96;
N. Kaldor, "A Model of Economic Growth," *Economic Journal*, LXVII
(1957), 595–96; or R. M. Solow, "Heterogeneous Capital and Smooth
Production Functions: An Experimental Study," *Econometrica*, XXXI (1963),
623–24.

up with the most inconvenient fact with which capital theory must contend, namely, that knowledge is both an input and an output in the production process. It is doubtful that we shall ever be able to "explain" technical progress to our own satisfaction since technical progress almost by definition involves the appearance of the unforeseen. We can only hope to devise a set of categories which will allow us to impose some order on our thinking about technical progress. Our use of a production function that combines two or more factors allows us to do this. (The problem of ordering our thoughts about technical progress would, of course, remain even if we decided to stick with capital as the only factor of production.)

Most economists would agree that technical progress occurs when the growth of knowledge allows us to get more income from a given quantity of the factors of production. But this consensus really supposes that we can define factors of production and agree upon the proper way of measuring their amounts. The trouble is that how we define and measure factors of production depends upon how we have organized our thinking about technical progress. Consider the problem of how to alter a simple production function in order to register the "fact" that technical progress has recently occurred.

Let
$$Y = GK^aN^b \tag{6}$$

where
$$Y = \text{income}$$
$$K = \text{capital}$$
$$N = \text{labor}$$
$$a + b = 1$$
$$G = \text{a constant}$$

To indicate that technical progress has recently occurred, we might increase the values of a and/or b in equation (6). This approach would not be very satisfactory. It destroys the useful "linearity" of our model since it would make the sum of a and b greater than unity. If carried far enough, it will produce a production function to which the law of diminishing returns does not apply—a preposterous result. (An example of a preposterous production function is $Y = KN$ where $\frac{\partial Y}{\partial K} = N$ regardless of the amount of capital used.)

Alternatively, we could say that technical progress is registered as an increase in the "quality" of capital or labor. But a change in quality, to the extent that it can be measured, *is* the numerical equivalent of some change in quantity. A more efficient labor force is really "more" labor. Nothing is to be gained by saying that income has increased because the advent of new knowledge has mysteriously increased the supply of labor or capital.

We are left with the option of registering technical progress by increasing the value of G in equation (6). This way of dealing with technical progress has become the accepted, though not the always acknowledged, practice in modern economics. It is worth examining for the light that it casts on our assumptions about the role of knowledge in production.

To the extent that we let G denote the "state of technology," we assign roughly the same role to knowledge in the production process as we do to a favorable climate. Production cannot take place without it. Once created, knowledge is open to all entrepreneurs without cost and is not diminished by use or the passing of time. For if knowledge is not free to all entrepreneurs, it is a scarce "resource" that commands a reward. If diminished by use or the passage of time, it will "eventually" become a scarce resource even though it is "now" free.[4] Of course not all knowledge falls into this category. Knowledge that is privately appropriated can, for purposes of organizing our thinking about technical progress, be viewed as part of the capital stock ("intellectual capital"), as part of the labor supply ("skilled labor") or as a separate factor of production. It cannot, however, be viewed as lurking behind "G" in the production function.

How useful is the assumption that "G" in equation (6) stands for the state of technology? Clearly the utility of this assumption—the premise that knowledge, like climate, is both freely available to all entrepreneurs and indestructible —depends upon the time perspective chosen. In the short run, no entrepreneur need pay anything to gain access to knowledge of the multiplication tables. This knowledge is in the possession of (almost) every worker that he hires and is not diminished by use or the passing of time. In the long run, this knowledge is a part of the human capital that is created by investment and destroyed, if not by use, at any rate by time. For to say the obvious: the skills of arithmetic are preserved and perpetuated only because society invests in the training of the young and so contains the invasion of the barbarians that never ends. Knowledge of the multiplication tables can be treated as a resource that is freely available in the short run only because the investment in education is heavy enough to make it nearly universal.

In fine, there is no objection to assuming that "knowl-

[4] The view that technology can be considered "inexhaustible" capital as distinct from the set of tangible assets that constitute exhaustible capital is elaborated in W. S. Vickrey, *Metastatics and Macroeconomics* (New York, 1964), pp. 33–36.

edge" or "the state of technology" is something different from capital and labor. But the assumption must be justified by its usefulness, not by an appeal to nature. Whether production functions exist in the real world, or whether they are, like perfect squares and circles, creations of our imagination, is another of the questions best left to philosophers. What is certain is that every production function that has been used by an economist has assumed a classification of the factors of production for which only limited validity can be claimed.

Technical Progress versus Investment as a Source of Growth

As a matter of observation we know that economic progress (however defined) entails the use of an existing set of men and machines to build a better set of men and machines. The metamorphosis of inferior into superior capital assets presupposes either the utilization of knowledge in existence but not previously applied or the simultaneous creation and application of new knowledge. Either way, economic progress occurs with the creation of new machines and labor skills, and it would seem to be an impossible task to decide how much of any given increase in income should be credited to technical progress as against increases in capital stock and labor supply. A quantum of knowledge usually has little or no economic payoff until it is "incorporated" or "embodied" in a set of specialized men and machines. One might say that income is increased by the growth of knowledge which makes possible the creation of better men and machines. Alternatively, one might say that income is increased by investment in men and machines who are specialized to make use of the growth of knowledge. One statement is as true as the other; taken together they suggest the logical impossibility of isolating the contributions of investment and technical progress to income growth.[5]

Still, problems of methodology which drive philosophers to despair merely inspire statisticians to greater ingenuity. (If it were otherwise, nothing would ever be measured.) And in recent years, several efforts have been made to measure the respective contributions of investment and technical progress to income growth. Most have involved assuming that, at any moment in time, the relation between income, capital, and labor satisfies equation (6); that is, that $Y = GK^a N^b$ where $a + b = 1$.[6] Numerical values are substituted for Y, K, a, and b for different years, and technical progress—"the multiplicative improvement factor"—is identified with the change in G or some function of the change in G.[7] In such studies, technical change is, in effect, "wholly organizational" in that it does not require the construction of new type capital assets. They permit the inference that income would be increased by an increase in knowledge even though gross investment were zero.

Studies which use this approach find that most income

[5] For a similar view of the relation of technical progress to investment, see L. L. Pasinetti, "On Concepts and Measures of Changes in Productivity," *Review of Economics and Statistics*, XLI (1959), 270–82. Pasinetti argues that "since capital comes from the production process itself, *on which technical change operates*, it cannot be dealt with in the same way as labor and land."

[6] Notably, S. Valavanis, "An Econometric Model of Growth, U.S.A. 1869–1953," *American Economic Review*, VL (1955), 208–21; R. M. Solow, "Technical Change and the Aggregate Production Function," *Review of Economics and Statistics*, XXXIX (1957), 312–20; O. Aukrust, "Investment and Economic Growth," *Productivity Measurement Review* (February, 1959), pp. 35–50; B. F. Massell, "Capital Formation and Technological Change in United States Manufacturing," *Review of Economics and Statistics*, XLII (1960), 182–88.

[7] In statistical work the variables in equation (6) are usually treated as functions of time and the relationships expressed as $Y(t) = Ge^{\lambda t} K(t)^a N(t)^b$. Technical progress is taken as measured by the value of λ.

growth is the result of technical progress, a conclusion that is not surprising since no allowance is made for improvements in the "quality" of men and machines. According to one such study, roughly 90 percent of the increase in output per man-hour that occurred in the manufacturing sector of the American economy between 1919 and 1955 should be ascribed to technical progress.[8] It implies that, if the fraction of national income invested annually in the United States were to rise from 10 to 20 percent, the rate of increase in national income would rise from 3 to just under 4 percent. This rise would represent a substantial increase in the annual growth rate (nearly one-third) and cannot be dismissed cavalierly. Nevertheless, the cost of greater growth in terms of current consumption sacrificed strikes most observers as high enough to cast doubt on the view that the electorate would choose greater growth on these terms if only it knew the facts.

This downgrading of the role of investment in economic growth has been challenged with two lines of criticism. One contends that in reckoning the contribution of investment to economic growth, allowance should be made for investment in human beings as well as machines. The effect of this correction is, of course, to revise upward our estimate of the rate at which the supply of labor increases over time. Thus, while the labor ingredient in the production function is usually measured by total hours worked, with psychiatrists and janitors being treated as interchangeable units for statistical purposes, E. F. Denison has devised an index of total labor input that registers changes in labor efficiency. The use of this index appreciably raises the contribution of

[8] Massell, "Capital Formation and Technological Change in United States Manufacturing," p. 187.

investment to economic growth.[9] For by Denison's calculations expenditures on education between 1929 and 1957 raised the quality of an hour's work—and hence the amount of labor input—by nearly 30 percent.[10]

The other counterattack in defense of the view that investment is a major source of economic growth asks for the use of more realistic production functions. According to one reasonable suggestion, all technical progress should be viewed as embodied solely in new machines; so that the efficiency of a machine built before, say, January, 1965, is not raised by an improvement in technology that occurs after January, 1965.[11] By this view gross investment is the process which transforms an increase in knowledge into more income—it is the "vehicle of technical progress." A growth model of embodied technical progress is examined in Appendix B.

The apparent effect of regarding technical progress in this way is to increase the importance assigned to the role of investment in economic progress since, at the limit, no gross investment, no increase in income. Still, so far as their policy implications are concerned, the differences between the two views of technical progress noted above are easily exaggerated.

Other things being the same, i.e., K, N, and G in the production function, the addition to next year's income from an increase in the fraction of income invested this year will be greater in a growth model where all technical progress requires the construction of new type machines

[9] *The Sources of Economic Growth in the United States and the Alternatives before Us.* Supplemental Paper No. 13, Committee for Economic Development (January, 1962).

[10] *Ibid.*, p. 85.

[11] Solow, "Investment and Technical Progress"; B. F. Massell, "Investment, Innovation, and Growth," *Econometrica*, XXX (1962), 239–52.

than in one where all technical progress is organizational. For technical progress that is organizational operates on the whole capital stock while embodied technical progress operates only on gross investment, hence, the marginal productivity of investment is higher in the latter case. The shorter the useful life of a machine and the greater the fraction of old machines in the population of capital assets, the greater the yield on an incremental outlay for new machines. However, when technical progress is embodied in new machines, an increase in investment operates to raise income by modernizing the capital stock, a process which must come to an end. New machines become old machines, and the day will come when the average age of capital assets cannot be further reduced without another increase in the fraction of income invested.[12]

In conclusion, we note that whenever the contribution of technical change to economic growth is measured with the aid of a production function, the statistical estimate is always the residual that cannot be explained by increases in capital and labor. And "like any residual, it picks up errors in all other estimates insofar as these are not off-setting." [13]

Summary

In recent years, models of economic growth have been used to throw light on some previously unsuspected relationships among savings, income, labor supply growth, capital formation, and the marginal productivity of investment. In particular, they have been used to show that, if labor is viewed as a factor of production distinct from capital, then

[12] E. S. Phelps, "The New View of Investment," *Quarterly Journal of Economics*, LXXVI (1962), 548–67.
[13] Denison, in *The Sources of Economic Growth in the United States*, p. 229.

the growth rate of the labor supply *is* the equilibrium growth rate of capital stock and income flow. Growth models have been used to show that the equilibrium growth rate of capital stock and income flow is independent of both the marginal productivity of investment and the fraction of income saved. They have also been used in efforts to measure the relative contributions to income growth of investment and technical progress. Nevertheless, the advent of growth models has produced no new, blazing insights into the fundamental issues of capital theory and, indeed, cannot be expected to do so. We shall always have with us the inseparable problems of how the factors of production shall be classified, the properties of the production function specified, and our thinking organized about the role of knowledge in the production process.

CHAPTER 10   Interest, Investment,

and Risk

Chapter 4 expressed the wish that all references to "the rate of interest" could be expunged from elementary treatments of capital theory. By our definition an elementary treatment of capital theory is one in which all investors possess the gift of perfect foresight, so that the outcome of every investment decision is known in advance and the investment process is entirely free of risk. Chapter 4 demonstrated that, given this assumption, "the rate of interest" is a redundant expression being merely another name for the marginal productivity of investment (MPI). In elementary capital theory it also follows that "the rate of interest" is a term to be taken literally. There exists one—and only one—rate of interest. A word of explanation is in order in defense of this last proposition.[1]

"The Rate of Interest": Possible Meanings

Strictly speaking, the existence of a single interest rate to which the rates of return on all investments conform requires more than a premise that all investors have perfect

[1] Irving Fisher argued that "under the hypothesis of a rigid allotment of future income among different time intervals, there is nothing to prevent great differences in the rate of interest from year to year, even when all factors in the case are foreknown." *The Rate of Interest* (New York, 1907), p. 384.
One cannot say that Fisher is wrong. The postulate of a "rigid allotment of future income among different time intervals" merely excludes the possibility that, given enough time, an economy can so arrange its investments that the rate of return is everywhere the same.

foresight. It is also necessary that, in the long run, some fraction of certain types of capital assets can be transformed via the process of disinvestment into other types of capital assets. This fraction must be large enough to insure that ultimately all types of assets in the capital stock yield the same rate of return. In earlier chapters where the Crusonia model was employed, the problem of shifting capital assets from one form to another did not arise. Only one type of capital asset (Crusonia) was posited.

We might pause to note that, to secure a single rate of interest, we need not assume that capital is, in the long run, a malleable substance that can take any form. It is only necessary that some part of the capital stock is, in the long run, sufficiently unspecialized that the shift of manpower and materials made possible by the natural process of depreciation will equalize the rates of return on all different types of capital assets.

In elementary capital theory "the rate of interest" may be a redundant and confusing term. As soon, however, as one progresses to any not-so-elementary treatment of capital theory, it acquires unique and useful connotations, though it does not, for this reason, cease to be a source of confusion. Let us therefore examine the more common meanings of the rate of interest and the relations they bear to the marginal productivity of investment (MPI).

When economists speak of *the* rate of interest they invariably mean one of four things (always assuming that they are not using the term as a synonym for MPI):

1) the set of interest rates at which capital assets are borrowed and lent, it being assumed that these different rates rise and fall together;

2) one particular interest rate in this set which is pre-

sumed to illustrate the behavior of all the rates, e.g., the
long-term rate of government bonds;

3) the average (weighted or unweighted) of all rates at
which capital assets are borrowed and lent;

4) the so-called "pure" rate of interest—that which
would be charged on a loan of capital assets entirely devoid
of risk for the lender.[2]

Each of these four meanings tacitly or explicitly assumes
a spread in the rates at which capital assets are borrowed
and lent. This spread can be attributed in small part to the
fact that different loans in the same amount have different
costs of production—that, for example, some borrowers are
easier to investigate for credit worthiness than others. But
economists commonly and properly attribute the spread of
interest rates mainly to the fact that, for the lender, different
loans carry different degrees of risk. The lender can suffer a
loss either because the borrower defaults in whole or in part
on the loan, or because the purchasing power of the commodity in which the loan is made (usually money) declines
before the loan is repaid.

Sometimes differences in interest rates are attributed in
part to differences in the "liquidity" of loan contracts
(IOUs). But one may doubt whether any good purpose is
served by trying to distinguish liquidity from risk. In a
world of perfect certainty, all loan contracts or IOUs would
be equally and perfectly liquid. At any moment, an IOU
that represents a claim to a sum payable in the future could
be sold for an amount equal to this sum discounted by MPI.

[2] In the real world, no loan of capital assets is ever entirely devoid of risk;
hence the "pure" rate of interest is an abstraction. It is, however, closely
approximated by the rate of return to be had by purchasing the bonds of a
reputable government that are shortly to be redeemed, e.g., by the yield
on United States bonds to be called next week.

It would not matter whether the sum were large or small. Nor would it matter whether the sum were payable tomorrow or a thousand years from tomorrow. In short, the spread of interest rates about an average is mainly interesting for what it reveals about two things: the willingness of individuals to accept the risks of investment, and the social arrangements in the form of corporations, banks, insurance companies, pawn shops, etc., that the economy has devised for spreading and shifting the risks of investment.

A Simple Model with Risk

Heretofore we have assumed that the investment process was wholly free of risk for the individual investor. In the first Crusonia model of chapter 4, MPI was seen to be the rate at which the capital stock would grow if consumption were zero and there were no diminishing returns to investment. This "natural" growth rate was a given condition of the problem. To show how interest rates are determined in an uncertain world, it is necessary to make one small change in this model. We shall no longer take the natural growth rate of the capital stock as given. Instead let us posit first that, for every Crusonia plant, different natural growth rates are possible; and second, that a probability estimate can be attached to each of these possible growth rates. We assume then a set of possible outcomes for every investment and assign a probability coefficient to each outcome. In short, we posit that MPI is what statisticians misleadingly call a random variable.[3]

Suppose, for example, that every investment has the six possible outcomes given in table 10.1; and that all are

[3] This chapter suggests one way of dealing with the existence of investment risk in the capital market. For a survey and critique of other ways, see J. A. Stockfisch, "Uncertainty, the Capitalization Theory, and Investor Behavior," *Metroeconomica*, VII (1955), 73–84.

TABLE 10.1

Investment Outcome (percent)	Probability Coefficient
8	1/6
6	1/6
4	1/6
2	1/6
0	1/6
−2	1/6

equally likely to be realized. From table 10.1 we can find the mathematical value of each outcome. This is simply done by multiplying each possible outcome by its probability coefficient. Thus the mathematical value of the highest possible rate of return on investment is 8 percent × $\frac{1}{6}$ or $1\frac{1}{3}$ percent. To obtain the mathematical value of MPI we sum up the mathematical values of its possible outcomes. Clearly the mathematical (mean) value of MPI as described by table 10.1 is $\frac{1}{6}(8 + 6 + 4 + 2 + 0 - 2)$ or 3 percent. Henceforth, the mathematical value of MPI will be designated by the conventional symbol $E(M)$.

Given the data on investment risks provided by table 10.1, we can begin to identify the determinants of the maximum, minimum, and average rates of interest in the set. Obviously the maximum rate cannot exceed 8 percent. Nobody will pay more than this rate to borrow capital since 8 percent is the highest possible rate of return that can be had by investing borrowed capital. By the same token, nobody will loan out any part of his own capital for a rate less than −2 percent. For a 2 percent loss is the worst outcome that can befall him should he invest directly. Thus the maximum and minimum values that MPI can take establish the upper and lower limits for the spread of interest rates.

The Taste for Risk, Insurance, and Lotteries

Will the spread of interest rates be as great as the spread of possible yields on investment? Not necessarily. The gulf between the maximum and minimum rates of interest will depend upon three additional factors: individual attitudes toward risk; the cost of organizing an insurance program for investors who dislike risk; and the cost of organizing a lottery for investors who prefer risk. By definition, an investor is anyone who owns capital assets.

Consider first the risk factor. We commence with the truth that a market for loans of capital assets comes into being when investors who dislike the risks of direct investment seek to shift them to investors who dislike them less. Risk is shifted by the purchase and sale of IOUs payable in the future. Without a market for loans, every investor must himself incur the risks set out in table 10.1. When he invests directly, six outcomes are possible. Each of these six outcomes he must risk in order to make an investment whose actuarial value is 3 percent.

Given a market for loans, the number of risk-bearing options open to the individual investor is vastly enlarged. Now when the lender parts with capital by buying somebody else's IOU, the risk of the venture is not governed entirely by "nature" as represented by the six investment outcomes of table 10.1. Risk to the lender can now be reduced in the same way that it is in the real world, that is, by requiring the borrower to post collateral. We shall return to this possibility presently. Before proceeding further, it is advisable to say a word on "the taste for risk."

Suppose an investor to be given a choice between an investment that carries the risks given by table 10.1 (where $E(M) = 3$ percent) and an investment that carries a sure and certain return of 3 percent. If he chooses the sure and certain return, the investor may be said to have an aversion to risk. If he chooses the more chancy investment, he may be said to have a preference for risk. The premium that the investor will pay to avoid or assume risk affords a statistical measure of this aversion or preference. Should every investor have neither an aversion to nor a preference for risk, there will be no spread of interest rates. If loans are made at all, they will be made at 3 percent—the mathematical value of MPI. In this circumstance, there is no good reason why a capital asset should be borrowed or lent. By the same token, there is no good reason why it should not be.

When, however, investors differ in their willingness to assume the risks of direct investment, a market for IOUs will emerge and with it a range of interest rates. Timorous (or prudent) investors sign away their rights to the better outcomes in exchange for a guarantee that preserves them from the worse outcomes. Bold (or foolhardy) investors secure the rights to the possibly better outcomes by providing the necessary guarantees.

Suppose that a lender's object is to eliminate entirely the risk of loss involved in parting with 100 units of capital (Crusonia) for one year. Suppose further that the loan can be made at 2 percent. By the terms of the loan, the lender will receive back 102 units at the end of one year. He can guarantee this result provided that the borrower is required to post 104.1 units of capital as collateral. The collateral can be the 100 units borrowed plus a margin of 4.1 units provided by the borrower. If the borrower is so unfortunate as to earn the minimum yield on capital of −2 percent, the collateral will still be 102 units at the end of the year. Let us be clear that this example of risk shifting is for the purpose of illustration only. The rate of interest that will actually prevail on loans entirely free of risk will depend upon the supply of and demand for them. Supply and demand will, in turn, be governed by the risks of investment, individual attitudes toward risk, the cost of insuring against the danger of loss, and the cost of operating lotteries.

One final word is in order respecting the taste for risk. To simplify our exposition, it is convenient to posit that the world is divided into people who have a taste for risk and people who have an aversion to it. In the real world no such division exists. The taste for risk is an operational concept and can only be inferred from the manner in which an investor behaves when given a choice of investment involving risk. With perfect consistency he may have an aversion to some risks and a taste for others which have the same mathematical expectation.[4] He may, for example, refuse to buy the common stock of a private corporation unless its yield is above that of safer government bonds, yet he may purchase a lottery ticket whose mathematical value is negligible because it carries the also negligible chance of a million dollar prize.

The foregoing discussion indicates that the principal *raison d'être* of "the capital market" is to shift risk from one investor to another. Although mainly a recitation of the commonplace, the discussion allows us to perceive several truths that are often overlooked—and sometimes pointedly ignored—in expositions of capital theory.

The first truth is that, in a world of investment risks and different tastes for risk, the number of different interest rates is virtually unlimited. The risk associated with any given loan can always be varied by changing the amount of

---

[4] On this truth see Jack Hirshleifer, "Risk, The Discount Rate, and Investment Decisions," *American Economic Review*, LX, No. 2 (1961), 112–16.

collateral required of the borrower. The number of different interest rates cannot exceed the number of loan contracts (IOUs) outstanding. Otherwise, the only restriction on this number is imposed by the limit to the divisibility of the commodities that are posted as collateral. This last restriction is really trivial; it merely means that if the collateral is United States currency, the amount specified must be some multiple of one cent.

The existence of a very great number of interest rates is worth underlining because it suggests the need for extreme caution in generalizing about the behavior of interest rates. This is true even when the analysis is conducted within the framework of our ultra-simple model. When the risks associated with investment are specified, we know the upper and lower limits of the set of interest rates. We do not know the actual range of interest rates in the set. Nor do we know the average of the rates at which loans are made. Moreover, we shall presently find that the assumption often made that, in the real world, all interest rates must move up and down together is quite wrong. It is an invitation to serious error to speak of *the* rate of interest. Indeed, there is a strong presumption that any writer—especially any writer on monetary theory—who speaks of *the* rate of interest is at least slightly confused.

We may establish a classification wherein IOUs are ranked according to the risks assumed by lenders. We may then glibly speak of an equilibrium set of interest rates and mean that, for each type of IOU, an interest rate prevails that equates the quantity supplied with the quantity demanded. But the demonstration of how this equilibrium is brought about is awkward and excessively time-consuming even when only two or three different types of IOU are assumed. This demonstration is reserved for Appendix C.

The above analysis also serves to show that there is no reason some interest rates in the set cannot at all times be zero or negative. And this conclusion holds even though individuals have a "taste for investment," $E(M)$ is above zero, and the stock of capital assets is growing. In fact, for most Western nations, the "pure" rate of interest—the rate on loans entirely free of risk—has often been below zero in the years since 1914. Negative rates of interest are usually attributed to the imperfect foresight of investors since they commonly occur in times of very rapid price inflation. But miscalculation need not be the only explanation.

The Role of Insurance

In our model the mathematical value of every investment is 3 percent, yet every investment carries the risk of a 2 percent loss. Should most investors have a strong aversion to risk, fear of the 2 percent loss is a force that *can* push the pure rate below zero. Whether fear of loss will actually have this effect depends upon the second factor that operates to reduce the range of interest rates. This factor is the cost of organizing a program to insure individual investors against loss.

Turn again to table 10.1. We can imagine any number of social arrangements that might be devised to protect the individual investor against some of the risks indicated in the table. The simplest type of insurance program would be an agreement among individual investors to pool the income from their several investments and divide it in proportion to the capital initially contributed by each investor. In other words they could organize a mutual fund. Conceivably, the cost of establishing an insurance program could exceed the difference between $E(M)$ and the lowest possible value of MPI. If so, the cost of investment insurance is, by definition, "prohibitive"; it reduces the prospective yield on the insured investment below what the minimum yield on an investment would be without insurance. In this circumstance, an insurance program will not be organized and the cost of insurance does not affect the range of interest rates.

A prohibitive cost of insurance represents one extreme. The other extreme is the possibility that the cost of insurance is zero. In this event, the *minimum* rate of interest at which loans are made is equal to $E(M)$ or 3 percent. The individual investor can guard himself against anything worse than a 3 percent return by joining the insurance program. Therefore, no one will loan capital for a return of less than 3 percent.

When the cost of insurance is zero, will the *maximum* rate of interest also be equal to $E(M)$? Not necessarily. We must, however, tread warily in answering this question. Should every investor have an aversion to risk, there is no range of interest rates when investment insurance has no cost. Nobody has to pay a premium to avoid risk. Nobody will pay a premium to assume a risk whose mathematical value is less than the return to be had by participating in the insurance program. In our example, participation in the insurance program guarantees a 3 percent return. Anyone who paid more than 3 percent to borrow capital would be gambling with the odds against himself. This possibility is excluded by the assumption that every investor has an aversion to risk. Given a universal aversion to risk, and an investment insurance program that has no cost, there is only one rate of interest. It is equal to $E(M)$.

The Role of Lotteries

Suppose that some investors are gamblers who will, if necessary, pay more than the mathematical value of a chance in order to obtain it. Suppose further that lotteries

are either illegal or have a prohibitive cost of operation, so
that investment is the only form of gambling open to investors with a taste for risk. Now even though insurance is
free, some investors will spurn safety in order to buy and
sell IOUs that promise a yield in excess of 3 percent. These
IOUs are perforce of low quality since they are not backed
by collateral sufficient to insure the promised rate of return.
Most people who buy them will be disappointed. Likewise,
most people who sell IOUs promising more than a 3 percent
return and (a most important qualification) post some of
their own capital as collateral will also be disappointed.
For by the given conditions of the problem, the yield on
borrowed capital can only average 3 percent. The division
of the actual—as distinct from the "contractual"—yield on
borrowed capital between borrowers and lenders will depend upon terms of the loan contract. Specifically, this division will depend upon the collateral posted, the contractual rate of return, and the conditions in which payment
must be made.

From the above argument we draw the following conclusion. If there are no lotteries, and if some investors have a
preference for risk, then a contractual rate of interest can go
as high as 8 percent—the best possible investment outcome.
Nobody will sell an IOU promising more than 8 percent
in order to obtain capital. He will obtain better odds by
using his own capital.

The picture is different if lotteries are legal and can be
organized without cost. Now gamblers can establish their
own games with any distribution of prizes they wish. Assuming that each game is fair, the purchase price of every
lottery ticket will be equal to the mathematical value of the
prize it promises. If the sums collected by the lottery in
ticket sales can also be invested in the riskless insurance

program at 3 percent, the mathematical value of the prize will actually exceed the purchase price by 3 percent. In this event, the maximum rate of interest on an IOU can only be 3 percent.

For purposes of pedagogical drill it is useful to analyze the connection between the marginal productivity of investment (MPI) and the set of interest rates on the extreme assumptions that the costs of providing insurance for investors and lotteries for gamblers are either prohibitive or zero. This we have done. Now let us base the analysis on the more realistic assumption that, while an insurance program is economically feasible, it has a cost. Bookkeepers, salesmen, securities analysts, tax specialists, and military heroes must be hired to run it. On this assumption, participation in the insurance program entitles one to a risk-free rate of return that is equal to $E(M)$ minus the cost of investment insurance. This net yield on capital committed to the insurance program perforce establishes the pure rate of interest. In our example, $E(M)$ is 3 percent. If the minimum cost of organizing an insurance program is always 2 percent of the capital assets involved, the pure rate of interest is 1 percent.

Now suppose that the cost of organizing a lottery is always equal to 4 percent of the sums collected; so that the yield on all sums spent on lottery tickets averages −4 percent. In this event, the maximum interest rate can exceed $E(M)$ by 4 percent. Thus the maximum rate of interest can be 7 percent.

Let us pause to review our findings. In a model where every investment outcome and its probability coefficient are given in table 10.1, the range of interest rates cannot extend upward beyond 8 percent nor downward beyond −2 percent. The range of interest rates that will actually prevail can be less than the spread of investment outcomes. It will be narrowed to the extent that individual investors have similar attitudes toward risk, and to the extent that the costs of organizing insurance programs for investors and lotteries for gamblers are low. It is impossible to say anything more specific about the connection between the range of interest rates and MPI viewed as a random variable.

In a Crusonia model characterized by risk, will the *average* rate of interest be above, below, or equal to $E(M)$? All three results are possible. Again the answer in any given case depends upon the attitudes of investors to risk, the cost of insuring against investment loss and the cost of operating lotteries. If most investors delight in risk taking and these two costs are high, the average of interest rates on loans will be above $E(M)$. Conversely, if most investors cringe before an uncertain future and these costs are low, the average rate of interest will be below $E(M)$. In the unlikely event that preferences and aversions to risk are normally distributed in the investing population about a mean that equals zero, the average rate of interest will also equal $E(M)$. If the economy has a strong aversion to risk, it is possible that the average rate of interest may be zero or negative even though $E(M)$ is positive.

Risk and Multiple Investment Opportunities

So far we have tacitly assumed that only one type of investment is possible in the sense that all investments carry the same risk and that MPI is a random variable. These postulates vastly simplify the task of making clear the tie between risk, capital productivity, and interest rates. Unhappily, the price of clarity is often distortion. Therefore, let us consider how this tie appears when more than one investment opportunity is allowed to the economy. We now assume that every investment opportunity is a unique random variable.

We perceive at once that the technique needed to reckon $E(M)$ is now much more involved since the economy is in a position to utilize different combinations of investment opportunities. The mathematical value of a given amount of investment depends upon the particular combination of investment opportunities utilized, and the manner in which a given capital sum is distributed among the set of investment opportunities in the combination chosen. One now has an $E(M)$ for every different investment "play." The greatest of these $E(M)$ is the relevant "mathematical value of MPI" for the economy. It can only be found by a tedious plotting and comparison of alternative investment plays.

Let N be the number of different investment opportunities open to the economy. Let T be the number of different ways in which N investment opportunities can be combined. Then,[5]

$$T = \binom{N}{1} + \binom{N}{2} + \cdots + \binom{N}{N} = 2^N - 1$$

But, of course, the computation does not end when a value has been found for T. The number of different values that $E(M)$ can take can be vastly greater than T. Indeed, this number is limited only by the number of parts into which a given investment sum can be divided. The reader can easily verify that, when the investment sum can be divided into four parts and two different types of investment

[5] This formula is derived in most modern textbooks on probability. See, for example, Frederick Mosteller, R. K. Rourke, G. B. Thomas, *Probability with Statistical Applications* (Reading, Mass., 1961), pp. 52–53.

can be made, the number of possible investment "plays" is five.[6]

Admittedly $E(M)$ is difficult to compute whenever the economy can make use of more than one investment opportunity. Still, $E(M)$ is the same phenomenon in a complex model as in a simple model. The main difference between the two models as regards the determination of interest rates lies elsewhere.

When only one type of investment is possible, MPI viewed as a random variable can be regarded as setting the upper and lower bounds to the set of interest rates. When the economy can invest in more than one way, the range of investment outcomes is increased. Once this range is very large, it ceases to restrict the dispersion of interest rates in any meaningful way (as, for example, when the best outcome is a 1000 percent gain and the worst outcome a 100 percent loss). In this situation, the minimum rate of interest is equal to $E(M)$ minus the cost of insuring investments. The maximum rate of interest is equal to $E(M)$ plus the cost of organizing a lottery.[7] In the real world, investment insurance programs are legal and well organized; lotteries are generally illegal and poorly organized.[8] Thus in the real world, the minimum rate of interest is known with a

[6] Let A and B denote the two types of investment open to the economy. If the investment sum S can be divided into four parts, the possible investment combinations are: $4A, 0B; 3A, 1B; 2A, 2B; 1A, 3B; 0A, 4B$.

[7] The cost of organizing a major lottery is not inconsequential. By one estimate, "approximately 20 percent of the total money wagered on British football pools, Irish Sweepstakes, and Norwegian lotteries is necessary to cover the commission and operating costs of the lottery." R. K. Kinsey, "The Role of Lotteries in Public Finance," *National Tax Journal*, XVI (1963), 18.

[8] It has been argued that, in some underdeveloped countries where lotteries are legal and well organized, gambling constitutes a serious impediment to investment. A recent United Nations study of economic development in Latin America is reported to have censored the native penchant for gambling on this ground. New York *Times*, April 7, 1963.

high degree of accuracy; the maximum rate of interest is known only to loan sharks and their victims—if it is known at all.

Interest Rates under Conditions of Risk

A cardinal tenet in most discussion of interest rates is that they all move up and down together and, hence, that no great violence is done to reality by talking about the behavior of *the* rate of interest.[9] (Instances in the real world where all interest rates do not move up and down together are usually attributed to the temporary "disorganization" of the capital market.) For some purposes this assumption may be justified as, for example, in speculation about the effect of interest rate changes upon the willingness of people to hold money. Nevertheless, we should be clear that the tenet has no solid foundation in capital theory.

Given the risks of investment that make possible a spread of interest rates, any particular interest rate is a function of four variables—investment risk itself, the cost of insuring against unfavorable investment outcomes, the cost of organizing lotteries to accommodate gamblers, and the willingness of investors to accept risk. The first three variables are matters of technology; the fourth is a matter of taste. Let us examine each of them in turn with the aid of table 10.1.

Suppose that some technological development narrows the range of possible investment outcomes without, however, changing $E(M)$. As a consequence, the maximum rate of interest will fall, the minimum rate of interest will rise, and the average rate of interest will remain unchanged.

Now suppose that some other technical development re-

[9] At least one authority, however, has already suggested that the average and pure rate of interest may move in opposite directions when the aversion to risk increases. J. W. Angell, *Investment and Business Cycles* (New York, 1941), pp. 54–55.

duces the cost of insuring investments while leaving the information in table 10.1 unchanged. If this happens, the minimum rate of interest must rise since the demand for "safe" IOUs will fall as the alternative direct investment becomes more attractive. The maximum rate of interest will remain unchanged, for the odds on the best possible investment outcome are not affected by the technical development. The average rate of interest will rise because it is an average of maximum and minimum rates. Likewise, if the cost of organizing lotteries is reduced by technical change, the maximum rate of interest will fall, the minimum rate of interest will remain unchanged, and the average rate of interest will fall.

Finally, suppose that the disturbance to equilibrium is provided solely by changes in attitudes toward risk. Two such changes can be distinguished: the range of individual tastes for risk may change; the *average* willingness of investors to accept risk may alter. Here one must tread very warily indeed.

A change in the range of individual tastes for risk will not, by itself, affect the average rate of interest. It will only affect the proportion of IOUs whose yields closely approximate the average rate of interest. A narrowing of the range of tastes for risk will increase this fraction. A widening of the range of tastes for risk will decrease it.

A change in the range of tastes for risk may affect the maximum and minimum rates of interest, but it need not do so. As we have seen, the range of interest rates is limited by the range of possible investment outcomes, the cost of insuring against unfavorable outcomes, and the cost of organizing lotteries. Only one result is certain. A change in the range of tastes for risk will alter the proportions of different types of IOU exchanged in the capital market. A narrowing of this range will raise the fraction of "average risk" IOUs. An increase in this range will raise the fractions of high-risk and low-risk IOUs.

The effects of a change in the *average* taste for risk of investors are even more difficult to assess. A decline in the average taste for risk will always lower the average rate of interest (except in the unusual case where the cost of investment insurance is zero). It will lower the minimum rate only when the latter is above either the worst possible investment outcome, or $E(M)$ minus the cost of investment insurance—whichever of these two investment returns is higher. Should the economy develop a greater aversion to risk, the pure rate of interest *may* fall. But this result is possible if, and only if, the pure rate of interest is already above the relevant minima established by "objective" investment and insurance opportunities.

Risk and Capital Formation

So far we have been concerned with the effects of the economy's taste for risk on the structure of interest rates when the risks of investment are known. Before concluding it is advisable to relate the "taste for risk" to the "taste for investment." As far as the individual investor is concerned, the two phenomena are formally distinct. The gambler may finance his oil drilling adventures out of income laboriously saved. Then again he may finance them on borrowed capital and consume the whole of his income (though he must, of course, pledge some part of his own capital as collateral against that which he borrows).

Still, in a world of investment risk, the taste for risk and the taste for investment are closely related since the only way the economy (as distinct from the individual investor) can avoid the risks of investment is by not investing. As we have seen, the individual investor may avoid the risks of investment by joining an insurance program or buying IOUs. The economy has not these additional options. It can only consume or invest out of income.

In a world of risk, any development that causes the economy's collective aversion to risk to increase will cause the fraction of income invested to fall. The increased aversion to risk will also operate to lower the average rate of interest, and possibly the pure rate as well. But let us be clear on one important point and so avoid a pitfall that has claimed many distinguished economists. The fall in the average rate of interest or pure rate of interest does not, in any meaningful sense, "cause" the fall in the fraction of income invested.[10] The marginal productivity of investment viewed either as a constant or as a random variable is a determinant of investment. The rate of interest—average or pure—is not.

Measuring the Quantity of Capital

Economists are fond of maintaining that "the value of a capital asset is equal to the sum of its future payments discounted by the rate of interest." We have already seen that this proposition is unambiguously correct only in the special, risk-free, case where there are no diminishing returns to investment and the rate of interest is, therefore, constant over time.

---

[10] Sometimes economists assert that a fall in the interest rate will cause an *increase* in the fraction of income invested. This result is held to follow because the fall in the interest rate has made it profitable to undertake investments whose yields were formerly below the rate of interest. In chapter 11 we shall see that such reasoning is at worst wholly fallacious and at best has validity only if arbitrage in the capital market is highly imperfect. Here it will suffice to anticipate our major finding. When arbitrage in the capital market is effective, the fraction of income invested and interest rates are determined simultaneously by the same forces. Consequently, the changes in the interest rate cannot "cause" changes in the rate of capital formation.

In the Crusonia model, the size of the capital stock can be found by taking an inventory. In the real world, it is obviously impossible to measure the size of the capital stock in this way. One measures instead the "real value of the real capital stock" by discounting income because this is the only property of capital that can be measured. Thus, all attempts to estimate investment in men or machines necessarily involve the application of a discount rate to the expected future payments for the use of men or machines. But which discount rate?

If the investment function is a true random variable, the answer is easily given. There is risk for the single investment in the short run but no risk for all investments in the long run. Risk can be eliminated by taking advantage of the law of large numbers. In this circumstance, income will be discounted by a rate equal to $E(M)$. When the investment function is not a true random variable, the correct discount rate is not so easily found; indeed, there is now no indisputably correct discount rate. For now the investor must contend with uncertainty as well as risk.

Suppose that Crusonia plants are generally thought to have a positive growth rate but that, as yet, nobody knows what this growth rate is. In this situation, it is conceivable that Crusonia will be exchanged for IOUs payable in the future. If so, a set of interest rates is established. But since investor ignorance is total, the ratio at which Crusonia exchanges for IOUs can have no objectively rational foundation. At any moment a certain quantity of capital (Crusonia) "exists"; but its future productivity—and hence its future income—is unknowable.

With the passing of time, investors can compile statistics on the growth rates of Crusonia plants and form an *a posteriori* estimate of $E(M)$. If the future repeats the past, the set of interest rates will be linked to this statistically derived investment function in the manner already described. But unless the future exactly repeats the past, the passing of time *will not* show that investors have used the "correct" rate to discount IOUs payable in the future. Should investors collectively underestimate the productivity of the capital during the accounting period, the level of interest rates will be too low; and sellers of IOUs will realize windfall profits from the investment of borrowed capital. Conversely, should investors collectively overestimate the productivity of capital, the level of interest rates will be too high; and sellers of IOUs will suffer unanticipated losses.[11]

This truth has an important, if perhaps obvious, implication for statistical efforts that seek to measure "the quantity of capital" by discounting income. The implication is simply that, in a world of uncertainty (as distinct from risk), there is no such thing as an "ideal" discount rate which relates the sum of the future incomes of a capital asset to its purchase price. For the future incomes themselves cannot be known exactly.

The most that one can say is that, in empirical research, some discount rates promise better results than others. The capital market exists in order to allow the shift of the risks of investment from investors who dislike risk to those investors who dislike it less or even enjoy it. Therefore, one should not choose, as a discount rate, the highest or lowest rate of interest in the set. The highest and lowest rates will almost certainly diverge from the marginal productivity of investment that will prevail in the near future. These ex-

---

[11] Veteran readers will recognize the above treatment of windfall gains and losses as a refinement of the theory of profit that Fred Weston developed some years ago. "A Generalized Uncertainty Theory of Profit," *American Economic Review*, XL (1950), 40–60.

treme rates exist to serve the needs of the most timid and the most foolhardy investors. Most of the time the statistician will get his best approximation to $E(M)$ by selecting some average of interest rates in the set.

To the extent that uncertainty respecting the future can be quantified into estimates of investment risk, there exists a "marginal productivity of investment" that influences the consumption-investment decision of the economy. Statistically, MPI is an elusive thing. In the real world, its magnitude is never revealed directly but can only be inferred from the behavior of interest rates including yields on stockholders' equity.[12] When words are used with precision in capital theory, "income" is always discounted by the "marginal productivity of investment." But in the real world, the income of a capital asset—machine, consumer durable, or human being—is always discounted by a rate of interest taken from the capital market. The justification for this practice is simply that, in an organized capital market, every interest rate is an approximation to MPI.

Recapitulation

In this chapter the marginal productivity of investment (MPI) has been viewed as a random variable, i.e., as a variable that can take a number of different values whose frequency distribution is known. When MPI takes this form, there need be no such thing as *the* rate of interest. The efforts of individual investors to assume or avoid the risks of direct investment bring into being a market for IOUs secured in whole or in part by collateral. The risk involved in holding an IOU can be altered by varying the collateral that secures

[12] The case for using yield on stockholders' equity as a proxy for MPI is argued in C. B. Hoover, "On the Inequality of the Rate of Profit and the Rate of Interest," *Southern Economic Journal*, XXVIII (1961), 1–12.

it. There is no significant limit to the number of different interest rates that IOUs will carry.

Nevertheless, the range of interest rates cannot exceed the maximum and minimum values that MPI can take. And the range of interest rates can be limited further by the dispersion of tastes for risk and the opportunities available to individual investors to insure against investment losses or gamble by buying lottery tickets. The mathematical value of MPI need not—and probably will not—equal the average rate of interest. Rather the mathematical value of MPI will usually be above the average rate of interest, since most investors have an aversion to risk. Therefore the statement often encountered that "the rate of interest tends toward the marginal productivity of investment" cannot be taken literally. The correct formulation of this proposition is that a rate of interest can diverge from the mathematical value of MPI only within certain limits. These limits, as we have seen, are given by the range of values that MPI can take, the cost of investment insurance, and the cost of organizing lotteries.

Money and Interest

The Role of Money in Interest Theory

Over the years, most economists have accepted that changes in the supply of, and demand for, money are somehow related to changes in interest rates. Not a few have gone much further. They have argued that these monetary developments are the main "cause" of changes in interest rates. Economists who adopt this extreme view are also likely to assert that changes in interest rates which have a monetary origin are important in the real world because they affect consumption and investment. A fall in the average rate of interest is presumed to raise the fraction of income invested. A rise in the average rate of interest is presumed to have the opposite effect.

We shall not pause to explore or contemplate the difficulties inherent in any effort to define money. For our purposes, money may be taken as the set of assets against which all other assets are directly exchanged. In the modern American economy only two assets of any importance are found in this set—the demand deposits of commercial banks and currency issued by the federal government. (Examples of unimportant assets in the set are travelers' checks and the minor Canadian coins that freely circulate on the American side of the frontier.) For an unequivocal statement that interest is essentially a monetary phenomenon, we need look no further than a famous passage in J. M. Keynes.

The rate of interest is not the "price" which brings into equilibrium the demand for resources to invest with the readiness to abstain from present consumption. It is the "price" which equilibrates the desire to hold wealth in the form of cash with the available quantity of cash;—which implies that if the rate of interest were lower, i.e., if the reward for parting with cash were diminished, the aggregate amount of cash which the public would wish to hold would exceed the available supply, and that if the rate of interest were raised, there would be a surplus of cash which no one would be willing to hold. If this explanation is correct, the quantity of money is the other factor, which, in conjunction with liquidity-preference, determines the actual rate of interest in given circumstances.[1]

In this chapter we shall consider how far the leading versions of the monetary theory of interest can be reconciled with the theory of capital so far expounded in this book. Unhappily, this undertaking is more ambitious than one might guess at first glance. The postulates of "real" capital theory are few in number and can be stated in brief and unambiguous propositions. Moreover, most of what we need to know about real capital theory was long ago set down rigorously and lucidly by Irving Fisher. No comparable claims can be made for theories of interest which assign great importance to the role of money. Monetary theories of interest exhibit great variety in their choice of assumptions and weighting of variables—so much so that they sometimes seem flatly to contradict one another. In the discussion of monetary theories of interest that follows we center our attention on the features common to most

[1] *The General Theory of Employment, Interest, and Money* (New York, 1936), pp. 167–68.
In another place, Keynes described the rate of interest as "strictly speaking, a *monetary* phenomenon in the special sense that it is the *own-rate* of interest (*General Theory*, p. 223) on money itself, i.e., that it equalises the advantages of holding actual cash and a deferred claim on cash." "Alternative Theories of the Rate of Interest," *Economic Journal*, XLVII (1937), 245.

of them while recognizing that this procedure is inevitably unfair to those treatments that avoid the vulgar errors of the majority.

Again, a comparison of "real" capital theory with some composite monetary theory of interest is difficult because the two are based upon mutually exclusive assumptions. In real capital theory, all resources useful in production are always fully employed. At any moment, output can only be increased by investing income. In monetary interest theory no such assumption is made. Indeed, many economists have declined to believe that monetary interest theory can profitably be separated from the study of business cycles. Hence, in comparing the two treatments of interest, one must always take care to distinguish between those differences which follow from the presence or absence of the full employment postulate and those differences which follow because one treatment is right (within the framework of its own assumptions) and the other wrong.

For the reasons set down above, a comparison of real capital theory and monetary interest theory is a difficult and not particularly promising undertaking. In this chapter, it is undertaken mainly because monetary interest theory is useful for making clear one important feature of the investment process that might otherwise remain obscure—the relation between the rate of interest and the price level. An additional inducement is provided by the melancholy fact that monetary interest theory is the only interest theory that many young economists encounter in their training.

Money as a Factor in Capital Formation

Economists who assign a significant role to money in capital formation generally do so for one or more of the following reasons: 1) Money is a capital asset in the sense that productivity of nonmoney assets is affected by the quantity of money available to expedite exchange; 2) People are frequently victims of one or more money illusions. In making their decisions to buy and sell, work or remain idle, consume or invest, they fail to take account of recent changes in the purchasing power of money; 3) Prices and wages in the real world are not perfectly flexible; so that changes in the supply of, and demand for, money can affect not merely the price tags on goods produced but their physical outputs as well; 4) Changes in the quantity of money in existence, and changes in the willingness of people to hold it in preference to other assets, affect the rate of interest; and a change in the rate of interest affects the fraction of income invested.

That "money has utility" is a truth so obvious that it is scarcely worth mentioning. The direct barter of one nonmoney asset for another is a manifestly unsatisfactory way of conducting trade. Any shortage of money that compels resort to barter perforce reduces economic efficiency. Therefore, the rational economy will, if necessary, devote some fraction of its resources to the production of money.

In colonial America where the stock of money consisted mainly of a supply of miscellaneous British, Spanish, and French coins that was not always sufficient for "the needs of trade," the argument that money is genuine social capital was worth making. In the present day, when the stock of money consists mainly of paper currency and demand deposits—commodities that have no significant costs of production—the case for money as social capital is hardly ever heard. It is simply taken for granted. In a modern economy, the behavior of the money stock often leaves much to be desired; but it is almost never defective in the sense that a shortage of money compels resort to barter. So far as its utility is concerned, in any modern economy, money is a commodity analogous to sand or gravel. Its total utility is incalculable. Its marginal social utility is negligible in that consumer welfare cannot be perceptibly increased by an addition to the stock of money.

The social usefulness of money is a subject soon exhausted. The nature of the money illusion—and its consequences for economic welfare—requires a closer examination. The ultimate basis of a money illusion is the understandable inability or unwillingness of human beings instantaneously to relate changes in the price level to changes in their money incomes. In its baldest formulation, the case for the existence of a money illusion states that if an individual receives, say, a 20 percent increase in his money income while, at the same time, the prices of all things that he buys and sells rise by the same 20 percent, he does not immediately perceive the fact. Rather he will erroneously consider that the monetary disturbance that has produced this result has made him either better off or worse off; and, until he learns the truth, his economic decisions will be affected by this illusion.[2]

Economists usually assume that a rise in money income is more clearly and distinctly perceived than a corresponding rise in the price level; so that, in fact, the victim of the money illusion will think himself better off. Further, economists usually assume that as an individual's income increases, the fraction that he wishes to save also increases. If these two assumptions about economic behavior are correct,

[2] The finer points of the money illusion are described in Don Patinkin, *Money, Interest, and Prices* (Evanston, 1956), especially pp. 23–24, 58–59, 112–13.

an economy operating under the spell of the money illusion will always invest a larger fraction of its income than it would in the absence of such an illusion. These assumptions are plausible, and possibly even accurate descriptions of how many people react to changes in money prices and wages. However, they do not by any means exhaust the set of logical possibilities.

So far as the relation of real capital theory to monetary interest theory is concerned, two propositions respecting the money illusion are worth elaborating. The first is that, although the money illusion exists, it is not clear that it has any particular economic significance. The money illusion is especially probable whenever money prices and money incomes are radically disturbed after a long period of relative stability. Individuals have accustomed themselves to thinking in terms of "normal" prices and have difficulty in adjusting their computations to the changed situation. There is, however, no reason *a priori* why all individuals should be the victim of the same money illusion. Their miscalculations could largely cancel out as some individuals behave as if they were better off and others behave as if they were worse off. Even if most individuals in a time of rapid price changes succumb to the same money illusion, they are not likely to persist in error forever. If monetary disturbances continue for any considerable period most people will learn to make their consumption-investment decisions in the light of constantly changing money price and wage data. In short, while the money illusion may be real enough on occasion, it cannot for this reason alone be an important factor in capital formation. The economic significance of the money illusion depends upon how many people are being fooled most of the time and upon their predilection for the same sort of folly.

Second, we might observe that, provided the nature
and magnitude of the money illusion are specified, it can
be incorporated into real capital theory without difficulty. The existence of the money illusion is perfectly
compatible with the postulate of full employment. Given
full employment at all times, its only effect is to raise (or
lower) the rate of capital formation. (In fairness to writers
who attach importance to the money illusion, one should
note that they virtually never employ the full employment
postulate.)

Of the four reasons given above for believing that money
and the willingness of the public to hold it is a factor that
affects real capital formation, the third is easily the most
important. To say the obvious, in the real world wages
and prices are not perfectly flexible. In particular, the
policies of labor unions, minimum wage laws, and the
concern of employers for their public reputations nowadays
combine to make virtually impossible any cut in the money
wage rate. Any contraction in the money supply, or any
increase in the desire of people to hold money, must cause
the demand for labor to decrease. When the demand for
labor is falling, the real wage can be cut, if it can be cut
at all, only slowly by inflation and the tightening of labor
discipline. Therefore, when money wages are sticky, any
fall in "total spending" leads directly to unemployment.
The nature of the wage and price rigidities that "cause"
unemployment when total spending falls is, of course, a
subject too vast for this book. The task of discerning some
of the more important variables that influence capital
formation in a full employment model is tough enough.

What of the assertion that money plays an important
role in capital formation because changes in the supply of,
and demand for, money affect the interest rate? The an-

alysis offered in support of this assertion constitutes the
heart of what most economists regard as the monetary
theory of interest. It will receive most of our attention in
this chapter.

The Transaction Demand for Money

Every version of the monetary theory of interest worthy
of the name somewhere seeks to explain why there is a
demand for money, that is, why an individual desires to
hold some portion of his personal wealth in the form of
money.[3] A list of his motives for holding money could be
extended almost indefinitely. In recent years, it has become
the fashion to follow J. R. Hicks[4] and group these motives
under two main headings, the transaction demand and the
speculative demand. Whatever may be said against this
approach, it has the undoubted advantage of simplicity.
The transaction demand for money presents no serious
problem. It is rooted in the inconvenience of barter and is
required by the "fact" that every commercial transaction
involves the direct exchange of goods and services for
money. The speculative demand for money is not disposed
of so easily.

In some circumstances people may seek to hold more
money than is necessary to function conveniently in the real
world because they expect its purchasing power to increase
in the near future. In other circumstances the motive may
be fear that, in the near future, the values of the particular
assets which they can conveniently hold will fluctuate more
than the purchasing power of money. The expectations

[3] For an admirable discussion of how the idea of a demand for money
evolved see, J. C. Gilbert, "The Demand for Money: The Development of
an Economic Concept," *Journal of Political Economy*, LXI (1953), 144–59.
[4] "Mr. Keynes and the Classics: A Suggested Interpretation," *Econometrica*, V (1937), 147–59.

and apprehensions which combine to produce a demand for money in excess of transaction needs can be subdivided at great length. For our purposes, however, the important truth is the most general one. In the real world the speculative demand for money exists because the future prices of capital assets are unknown. This being so, an individual can implement his taste for risk by varying the fraction of his personal wealth that he holds in the form of money.

Most writers who attach importance to the role of money in the determination of interest rates stress that people commonly hold money in order to avoid the risks associated with the holding of other assets. They assume, in effect, that money is regarded as a safe "store of value." Clearly this assumption is valid only for particular times and places and does not apply to an economy that has recently experienced several decades of rapid inflation. For this reason, the view which emphasizes the holding of money as a way of avoiding risk fails to provide an acceptable perspective on the tie between money and interest rates.

So long as no one expects the purchasing power of money to change, the willingness of most people to hold money in excess of transaction needs signifies only one thing: a collective distaste for risk. But when there is no such expectation, a speculative demand for money is not conclusive evidence of a desire to avoid risk. Indeed, when the future prices of capital assets are uncertain, the holding of money is likely to be neither the most risky nor least risky of the options open to an investor. (By definition an investor is anyone who holds capital assets that he can consume, mortgage to buy more capital assets, or exchange for money.) An increase in the demand for money may represent a rise in the economy's collective aversion to risk. It may also represent the opposite. It is this ambiguity—the impossibility of positing an unchanging relation between the demand for money and the taste for risk—that makes monetary interest theory such a complicated, confusing, and unsatisfactory thing. Let us approach the complications by easy stages.

Consider first the transaction demand for money. At the outset one may fairly ask whether any meaningful distinction can be made between the transaction and speculative demands for money. In a world entirely free of risk, it is difficult to see why a demand for money should exist at all. If the future values of all capital assets were known with perfect certainty, any type of capital asset could serve as a *numéraire* that measures the value itself and of all objects.[5] As a *numéraire*, one type of asset would be no better and no worse than any other. It would be immaterial, that is, whether the measuring rod in exchange transactions was a bale of cotton, a bushel of wheat, or a ton of coal. Still, in the hope of distinguishing a genuine transaction demand for money let us assume a world entirely free of risk which, nevertheless, has a money commodity. Let us, in fact, employ the riskless version of the Crusonia model used in previous chapters and give it a stock of money.

Suppose that the marginal productivity of investment

---

[5] One writer has argued that, even in the absence of uncertainty, "a lack of synchronization between the receipt of income and its outlay would give rise to a need for cash-balances so long as there are not perfect facilities for the borrowing of money in anticipation of receipts and the investment of money during the period elapsing between receipt and outlay." A. W. Marget, "The Monetary Aspects of the Walrasian System," *Journal of Political Economy*, XLIII (1935), 160–61. The rebuttal to this argument would seem to be that, in the absence of uncertainty, there would be perfect facilities not so much for borrowing money (which might not be needed) but for exchanging IOUs. In such a world every IOU would have a known actuarial value.

(MPI) in terms of Crusonia units is a constant. (Once again no good purpose would be served by assuming diminishing returns to investment.) Suppose further that the economy has somehow come into possession of a quantity of indestructible silver dollars which, by common and universal consent, have become the stock of money. The assumption of a constant MPI in terms of Crusonia units can be taken as signifying that the stock of money is sufficient for "real" needs. That is, the rate of capital formation would not be affected by an incremental increase or decrease in quantity of silver dollars in circulation. We wish to set forth the relation of the demand for money to the rate of interest and the price level. Let

M = stock of money

K_0 = quantity of capital (Crusonia) existing now

K_1 = quantity of capital (Crusonia) existing one year from now

r = marginal physical productivity of investment

i = money rate of interest

a = fraction of income invested

b = fraction of wealth that every individual wishes to hold in form of money

P_0 = price of a unit of Crusonia in terms of money now

P_1 = price of a unit of Crusonia in terms of money one year from now

When values are assigned to M, K_0, r, a, and b, the values of K_1, i, P_0, and P_1 are easily found. Suppose that $M = \$100$, $K_0 = 200$, $r = 0.20$, $a = \frac{1}{2}$, $b = \frac{1}{5}$.

Then $(M + K_0)$ must, in terms of money, equal $\$500$, and K_0 must equal $\$400$. The money stock ($\$100$) is equivalent to 50 units of real capital; so that $P_0 = \$2$. During the year income on capital is rK_0, or in real terms, 40. Since $a = \frac{1}{2}$, the capital stock increases by the product, ar, or by 10 percent. Therefore, $K_1 = 220$ and $P_1 = \$1.82$.

Arbitrage insures that the (money) rate of return on investment is equal to the (money) rate of interest. One hundred dollars invested in Crusonia plants will grow to $\$109.20$ by the year's end. Thus, $i = 9.2$ percent, the formula for the money rate of interest being given by

$$i = \frac{(1 + r)P_1 - P_0}{P_0}$$

This method of demonstrating the relationships among capital stock, capital productivity, money supply, the demand for money, prices, and investment is awkward but useful. It shows clearly that:

1) A change in the supply of, or demand for, money affects the money rate of interest;

2) A change in the money rate of interest is the same thing as a change in the price level, specifically, a fall in the money rate of interest *is* a fall in the price level while a rise in the money rate of interest *is* a rise in the price level;

3) A change in the money rate of interest does not by itself affect the real rate of interest;

4) Therefore, a change in the money rate of interest does not by itself affect real consumption or real investment.

From the above analysis, it follows that, while variations in the transaction demand for money can affect the money rate of interest, such variations can affect the real rate of capital formation if, and only if, one or more of the following conditions are present: the money stock is inadequate for "the needs of trade," human beings are victims of some money illusion, or the prices of some capital assets or their services are sticky.

It does not follow that economists who attach importance to the transaction demand for money in the business world are wrong to do so. But the conclusions that they reach depend upon the set of economic institutions and investor attitudes that they posit. And since different writers make different assumptions, it is not surprising that they do not agree very closely on the role played by the transaction demand for money in capital formation. Moreover, economic institutions and investor attitudes change with distressing rapidity in the real world. Therefore, it would be unreasonable to expect that anyone will ever produce *the* definitive analysis of the role of the transaction demand for money in capital formation.

The Speculative Demand for Money

Our examination of the transaction demand for money has not yielded any very startling result. We merely found that when a transaction demand for money is incorporated into the "real" theory of capital developed in previous chapters, no important conclusion need be revised. To give importance to the transaction demand for money one must assume some other things as well. Depending upon what these other things are, the disturbance to real capital theory can be great or little. Let us hope that an examination of the speculative demand for money—the demand that exists because the future is uncertain—will prove more profitable.

In chapter 4 we eliminated risk for the individual investor by assuming that the natural growth rate of the capital stock was wholly predictable. In chapter 10 we assumed that every particular investment involved risk but that the amount of risk was measurable. Chapter 10 allowed the individual saver to reduce investment risk for himself in one or both of two ways. He could make use of the law of large numbers by joining with others to pool the risks of investment in an insurance program. Or he could loan capital assets to someone else and require that the borrower post a quantity of collateral that eliminated or reduced the risk of loss on the loan. When investment entails risk, a market for loans of capital assets will develop. With it will emerge a set of interest rates that reflect the risks involved in holding the different types of IOUs. The average of the interest rates in this set can be equal to, greater than, or less than the mathematical value of MPI.

Does the introduction of a speculative demand for money into our simple risk model of capital formation change it in any important respect? Not really. The existence of money merely allows the individual investor a third way of holding his personal wealth so as to reduce or embrace risk. Unhappily, this obvious, not to say trivial, truth has often been neglected with results productive of much confusion.

According to some authorities, the investor regards the holding of money as the alternative to holding IOUs and vice versa. Whenever he seeks to "save income," he offers part of his money stock in exchange for additional IOUs. Likewise, whenever he seeks to "consume capital," he offers part of his IOUs in exchange for additional money. It follows that an increase in the demand for money is the same thing as a fall in the demand for IOUs, i.e., the same thing as a rise in the average rate of interest. The confusion injected by this chain of reasoning into both real capital theory and monetary interest theory can scarcely be exaggerated.

The argument rests, of course, on an unacceptable premise. When the individual reduces his demand for money, he may buy IOUs. He may also offer part of his money hoard in exchange for real capital assets—land, buildings, washing machines, etc. Conceivably, he could offer all of the money that he wishes to discard in exchange for real capital assets. In this event, a fall in the demand for money would have no effect whatsoever on the demand for IOUs and, hence, no effect upon the average rate of interest. In the real world, an individual investor who seeks to reduce his stock of money will almost certainly do so by buying *both* IOUs and real capital assets. In this case, a fall in the demand for money will be associated with a rise in the demand for IOUs. But now it is not "the same thing" as a rise in the demand for IOUs. Thus one cannot say how an investor's decision to reduce his holding of money by, say, 20 percent will affect the demand for IOUs unless one knows his preference for additional IOUs as against additional capital assets.

Let us accept that, for all practical purposes, a change in the demand for money always produces some change in the demand for IOUs. Does it follow that the rate of interest must be affected? Does it follow, for example, that a fall in the demand for money which leads to the exchange of cash for IOUs must cause the rate of interest to fall? We shall presently see that the correct answer to this question depends upon two things—what is meant by "the interest rate" and the development that produced the change in the demand for money.

In chapter 10 we noted that the assumption of a single rate of interest is not appropriate to a world in which

investment is associated with risk. A simple model with
risk generates a set of interest rates whose upper and lower
limits can be known, but this set can contain as many
different interest rates as there are IOUs. In chapter 10
we also found that there was no reason why all of the
interest rates in the set should move up and down together.

Unhappily, the complications that would ensue if one
attempted to analyze the behavior of interest rates in the
real world on the assumption that they do not move up
and down together are so formidable that the experiment
has never been tried. *The* rate of interest is nearly as firmly
entrenched in monetary interest theory as in the riskless
world of Frank Knight. Most commonly when monetary
theorists speak of the rate of interest they mean either the
pure rate of interest (that prevailing on riskless loans) or
some average of interest rates. For the reasons developed
in chapter 10, the pure rate and the average rate may move
in the same direction but need not do so. When the demand
for money is changing, it is most unlikely that these two
rates will move in the same direction.

The reasons that explain why people normally hold more
money than is necessary to escape resort to barter apply
with equal force to such relatively safe IOUs as saving
bank deposits, saving and loan association deposits, and
short-term government bonds. Thus it is virtually impossible that an increase in the speculative demand for money
should cause a decrease in the demand for these safe
IOUs. Hence, a shift from IOUs "in general" to money
almost never raises the pure rate of interest. When an
economist asserts that a rise in the demand for money
operates to raise the rate of interest one should, in all
charity, assume that he has in mind some average rate of
interest.

Yet so great is the confusion on economic fundamentals in monetary interest theory that even the validity of this charitable interpretation cannot be taken as self-evident. As long as the provision of an insurance program for investors has a cost, any decline in the economy's willingness to accept risk will be registered by a fall in the average rate of interest. If the purchasing power of money is expected to remain largely unchanged in the near future, a flight from risk will show up as increase in the demand for money. But according to one influential version of monetary interest theory, this increase in the demand for money has precisely the opposite result. It produces a rise in the average rate of interest.

This difference of opinion serves to point up the most serious omission in the monetary theory of interest—the tendency to center attention on the demand for IOUs while neglecting the forces that govern their supply. Actually, the supply of, and demand for, IOUs are determined by the same thing—the desire of individuals to avoid or assume the risks involved in holding real assets. Any development that serves to raise the demand for money and relatively safe IOUs will concomitantly operate to reduce the demand for not-so-safe IOUs. Admittedly the representative investor at any given moment is both a borrower and a lender in the sense that he has purchased the IOUs of other investors and sold some of his own. But the representative investor, if he is rational, will never simultaneously buy and sell IOUs that carry the same amount of risk. Such a transaction would be pointless. Therefore, if the willingness of most investors to buy low-risk IOUs increases, it follows that their willingness to sell high-risk IOUs in order to obtain the use of additional real capital assets has decreased.

In the light of the above remarks let us consider again the assertion that a rise in the demand for money will cause the average rate of interest to rise. If one assumes that the risk associated with every given investment is known to all potential investors, that individual differences in the taste for risk produce both a market for IOUs and a speculative demand for money, and that the supply of money is given, then the assertion is dead wrong. An increase in the speculative demand for money is merely one manifestation of a flight from the risks associated with direct investment and/or the holding of high-yield IOUs.

Admittedly the fall in the demand for high-yield IOUs is a force tending to raise the average rate of interest on all IOUs. At the same time, the search for safety is manifested as increase in the demand for low-yield IOUs and so tends to lower the average rate of interest. The crucial consideration here is the truth already noted, namely, that the supply of, and demand for, IOUs are governed by the same thing—the willingness of investors to accept the risks involved in holding real assets. Hence, the search for safety increases the ratio of low-yield IOUs to high-yield IOUs and, in this way, drives down the average rate of interest.[6]

We might pause here to emphasize that the supply of IOUs differs in one crucial respect from both the supply of money and the supply of real assets. It is not unreasonable to assume that, in the short run, the supply of money is fixed by government rules or banking policy. We know that the supply of real assets can only be increased by

[6] In fairness, it should be mentioned that many monetary theorists have only the very short run in mind when they argue that an increase in the demand for money will cause a rise in the average rate of interest. See, for example, J. W. Angell, *Investment and Business Cycles* (New York, 1941), pp. 54–55.

investment. But given the freedom of contract that makes possible a capital market for IOUs, the supply of IOUs can vary in response to changes in the taste for risk or subjective estimates of risk even though the supply of money and real assets remains fixed. An increase in the demand for money must produce a rise in the average ra e of interest only on the assumption that the supply of IOUs is fixed, and such an assumption blatantly contradicts the assumption that individuals are free to trade risks in a capital market.

Suppose that we take leave of our manageable Crusonia model and regard the real world. Should we still assert that an increase in the demand for money will never produce a rise in the average rate of interest? Obviously not. Buyers and sellers of IOUs do not always estimate the risks of direct investment in the same way, and, in the real world, the supply of money is itself a variable. We might digress to note that it is practically impossible to reckon the average rate of interest from empirical data. We have only a hazy idea of the average rate of interest on install- ment credit contracts given the innumerable devices that lenders employ to disguise the interest payment. We have scarcely any idea at all of the interest rates exacted by loan sharks on the Brooklyn waterfront. Therefore, no good purpose is served by speculating whether "in reality" an increase in the demand for money ever causes *the* average rate of interest to rise.

We can only say the obvious. An increase in the demand for money has often been associated with a rise in the yield on certain classes of IOUs, e.g., bankers' acceptances. The economic consequences of these particular associations may —or may not—be significant for the study of business cycles. Either way, there is no good reason why a theory of interest that aspires to generality should be concerned

with them. A preoccupation with the effect of a change in
the demand for money on a particular subset of interest
rates may be a worthy thing in a central banker who can
by his action directly influence these rates. Such a preoccupation is a positive handicap to anyone who wishes to
understand how the marginal productivity of investment,
the taste for investment, and the taste for risk interact to
determine consumption, investment, and the terms on
which IOUs "in general" are bought and sold.

The Interest Rate and Investment

What of the proposition firmly embedded in most versions of the monetary theory of interest that a fall in the
average rate of interest will cause investment to increase?
We know that, when the investment process is presumed
to be entirely free of risk, this assertion is either false or
superfluous. If there are no diminishing returns to investment, it is false. MPI, and hence the rate of interest, never
changes. If there are diminishing returns to investment,
the proposition is superfluous. For "diminishing returns"
is, by definition, a fall in MPI as investment increases.

If investment is associated with risk, the proposition that
a fall in the average rate of interest will cause investment
to increase is still wrong. But now its error is not so obvious. The proposition rests on the argument that a fall
in the average rate of interest will encourage investors to
borrow capital in order to undertake investments whose
prospective returns were formerly below the rate of interest but are now equal to or above it. This argument
must be rejected. It fails to recognize that the average rate
of interest is largely governed by MPI and can diverge
from MPI only to the extent that costs must be incurred

to organize insurance programs for investors and lotteries for gamblers. As noted in chapter 10, a decline in the average rate of interest, the mathematical value of MPI remaining unchanged, can signify only one thing: a decrease in the rate of investment. The single investor may shift the risks of investment to others by holding money or low-yield IOUs. These two options are not open to the economy which can only reduce the risks of investment by not investing. To say that an economy's taste for risk has declined is merely another way of saying that its taste for investment has declined.

A Perspective on Monetary Interest Theory

As long as capital formation is analyzed on the premise that all resources are, at all times, fully employed, nothing is gained by treating the supply of, and demand for, money as significant economic variables. Given the full employment postulate, a preoccupation with the role of money in the investment process is not only unrewarding; it is positively pernicious, since it causes one to lose sight of the more fundamental forces at work. Individual investors hold money in excess of their everyday transaction needs in order to assume or escape risk. They buy and sell IOUs for the same reason. In "pure" capital theory, the important and inclusive variable is "the taste for risk," not the supply of, and demand for, money.

On the assumption that full employment always exists, a monetary theory of interest would seem to have only the negative and limited value discerned earlier in this chapter. It can be used to show that changes in the purchasing power of money, the price level, and the money rate of interest have no effect whatever on capital formation. We may conclude that the only monetary theory of interest worth bothering about is that which is inextricably bound up with the study of business cycles.

Over the years several ambitious efforts have been made to bridge the gap between "real" capital theory as expounded by Böhm-Bawerk, Fisher, and Knight, and monetary interest theory as it evolved, especially in Britain, from Marshall through Keynes and Pigou to Hicks. These efforts have produced, in addition to an abundance of turgid prose, many ingenious refinements in both areas but not much genuine integration.[7] One can make a good case that this larger endeavor was doomed to failure from the start by the logical impossibility of reconciling speculations about capital formation that proceed from mutually exclusive postulates. Thus, prices and wages are perfectly flexible or they are not. Full employment always exists or it does not. No amount of ingenuity will suffice to "integrate" the work of authors who do not agree on this all-important point of departure.

Still, monetary interest theory ought not to be criticized because it cannot be reconciled with real capital theory. It has its own, different goals. In the real world, prices and wages are not perfectly flexible, unemployed resources are a problem, money illusions exist, and borrowers and lenders differ not only in their tastes for risk but also in their subjective evaluations of risk. The need for hard thinking about the role of money in capital formation can be taken as self-evident. Rather, monetary interest theory is open to criticism because its underlying assumptions are seldom made clear. If its main object is to illuminate the workings of the capital markets, it must specify with

[7] The most recent addition to the list of distinguished failures is, of course, Don Patinkin, *Money, Interest, and Prices.*

precision what is assumed about the degree of price and wage rigidities, the type of money illusion, and the psychological differences of borrowers and lenders. This, alas, is seldom done except in those monetary treatments of interest that are unashamedly "institutional" and seek only to show how common and recurring developments affect the yields on government bonds, "prime commercial paper," common stocks, etc.

Shall we accept Frank Knight's counsel[8] and reject as hopeless economic theory any assertion that "interest is mainly a monetary phenomenon"? Almost, but not quite. If the assertion is interpreted literally it is, of course, absurd. The phenomenon of interest is traceable to the productivity of investment, the taste for investment, and the existence of risk for the individual investor. These ultimate sources of interest are, so to speak, "facts of nature" which have nothing to do with the presence or absence of money. However, writers who hold that interest is mainly a monetary phenomenon generally have something else in mind. Sometimes they only seem to say that short-run changes in interest rates can be traced to changes in the supply of, and demand for, money. We have no quarrel with this view. One could, with equal truth and greater generality, say that short-run changes in interest rates can be traced to changes in the supply of, and demand for, IOUs. Alternatively, writers who make interest mainly a monetary phenomenon do so to stress that, since a central bank can control the supply of money, it can decree, within wide limits, what certain interest rates shall be. The evaluation of this claim is an undertaking too vast for this book. Suffice it to say that the claim is valid to the extent that "the capital market is riddled with imperfec-

[8] *On the History and Method of Economics* (Chicago, 1956), pp. 221–26.

tions, so changes in the supply of credit at one corner of the market will not spread across it evenly."[9]

At the limit of the perfect capital market, the central bank is entirely devoid of any function. In such a market its policies could have no effect on relative prices. Given the imperfect capital market of the real world, the central bank seeks to make use of the imperfections to do good and, in the opinion of most economists, succeeds more often than it fails. Nevertheless, the art of central banking is possible only because the central bank can alter the supply of money more rapidly than individuals and institutions can adjust to the resulting price changes imposed upon them. Since the subject matter of monetary interest theory is money, central banking, investor psychology, and the imperfections of the capital market, it is unlikely ever to achieve outstanding rigor or universality. This is not a matter for regret. Monetary interest theory justifies itself to the extent that it improves the art of central banking.

[9] A. G. Hart and P. B. Kenen, *Money, Debt, and Economic Activity* (3d ed.; Englewood Cliffs, 1961), p. 445.

CHAPTER I 2   Capital Curiosa

The history of economics contains many curious things. Some incorporate error that once passed for truth; others are the first awkward, not wholly accurate, formulations of important propositions. In most parts of economics these curiosities have been consigned to the undusted rooms of the library to be studied by specialists in the history of ideas. Not so in capital theory.

Three Unfortunate Survivals

Here, not a few curiosities that long ago should have met this fate survive to perpetuate intellectual confusion. In self-defense, the economist ought to be familiar with three especially troublesome survivals. They are: 1) the view that "abstinence" or "waiting" is a separate factor of production that commands a reward; 2) the period of production; 3) zero and negative rates of interest.

Waiting as a Factor of Production

In the history of capital theory, the ideas of waiting and the period of production are closely related. The first formulation of both ideas probably lies somewhere in the usury controversy of the Middle Ages. By the end of the nineteenth century, they had been explicitly enunciated and given an important place in capital theory. Nineteenth-century economists observed that the construction of virtually every useful thing required time, that workers who were employed in the construction of useful things were paid continuously and consumed continuously, and that capitalists who financed workers during the period of production collected interest and profit.

These observations were, of course, entirely correct. But in the works of influential authors, most notably Nassau Senior, John Stuart Mill, and Alfred Marshall, they were made to support the objectionable inference that interest and profit is the reward that capitalists claim because they abstain from consumption during the period of production.[1] To use the simile favored by some writers, capitalists receive interest and profit because, being either richer or more patient than workers, they are willing to wait while a given quantity of present consumption "ripens" via investment in capital goods into more consumption in the future. The most uncompromising statement of the view that "interest is payment for waiting" we owe to Gustav Cassel.

Supposing a set of workmen have built a house, they may themselves wait for the money that the use of the house will bring in year after year for a long time to come. But they may be not willing to do so; they may prefer to get the reward of their labour at once; in this case they may find another person willing to take over the function of waiting in their place. This man will then buy the house; the workmen will immediately get their wages; and the buyer will settle down to wait. This shows that waiting is a quite separate function of economic life. It may be taken over by anyone who chooses to do it; but there can be no doubt about the fact that somebody must do it.[2]

[1] Senior, *An Outline of the Science of Political Economy* (London, 1836), pp. 153-54; Mill, *Principles of Political Economy*, Ashley, ed. (New York, 1909), pp. 31-33; Marshall, *Principles of Economics* (8th ed.; London, 1920), pp. 230-35.
[2] *The Nature and Necessity of Interest* (London, 1903), p. 87.

Cassel is here a victim of his terminology. He is merely saying that a capital asset during its lifetime yields a surplus of services greater than its cost of construction, and this surplus accrues to somebody. This surplus, which Cassel calls interest, is another name for what this book has, with fair consistency, called income. Thus income (or interest) is the reward one receives for not consuming capital and an addition to income (or interest) is what one receives for not consuming income (or interest). Therefore, waiting is not a separate factor of production. It is only another name for production itself. The statement that interest is payment for waiting or abstinence is not so much wrong as tautological.

As for waiting and the period of production, we have already seen with the aid of Crusonia models that a rate of interest will exist even though every act of investment yields a consumable product "immediately." To the individual investor, the creation of capital assets and the purchase of IOUs are acts that serve the same purpose: they allow him to increase his income by sacrificing consumption. And arbitrage will keep the rate of interest equal to the marginal productivity of investment provided, of course, that investment outcomes are known with perfect certainty.

While the defense of waiting as a separate factor of production offered by Cassel is seldom found in modern treatments of capital theory, the concept is not quite dead. Recently Robert Dorfman has provided a more rigorous defense that goes as follows: Assume that

(a) Labor is the single, "ultimate" factor of production.
(b) During some period of production labor is applied continuously to a "thing" available without cost which, at the end of this period, emerges as a con-

sumable product. This is equivalent to positing that
capital consists entirely of unfinished consumption
goods.

(c) The flow of consumption goods per unit of time can
be increased, beginning at some time in the future,
by lengthening the period of production.

(d) An increase in the period of production entails some
temporary reduction in the flow of consumable products.

(e) There are diminishing returns to investment.[3]

Write Y for consumable products per unit of time, N for
the number of workers, and p for the length of period of
production. The above assumptions imply that

$$Y = f(N, p) \tag{1}$$

$$\frac{\partial Y}{\partial N}, \quad \frac{\partial Y}{\partial p} > 0 \tag{2}$$

and

$$\frac{\partial^2 Y}{\partial N^2}, \quad \frac{\partial^2 Y}{\partial p^2} < 0 \tag{3}$$

Necessarily, $\frac{\partial Y}{\partial N} < \frac{Y}{N}$; hence $Y > \left(\frac{\partial Y}{\partial N}\right) N$. Therefore, if
labor N is paid at a rate equal to its marginal productivity,
$\frac{\partial Y}{\partial N}$, there is a surplus, $Y - \left(\frac{\partial Y}{\partial N}\right) N$, that remains after
labor has been compensated.

[3] "A Graphical Exposition of Böhm-Bawerk's Interest Theory," *Review of
Economic Studies*, XXVI (1959), 153–58; "Waiting and the Period of Production," *Quarterly Journal of Economics*, LXXIII (1959), 351–72. Strictly speaking, conditions (d) and (e) are not independent assumptions but corollaries
that can be deduced from conditions (a), (b), and (c). Condition (d) is
present because, when the supply of labor and the stock of unfinished consumption goods are given, any increase in the period of production will
postpone the day on which each unfinished consumption good in the existing
stock becomes a final product. Condition (e) is present because, if there
are no diminishing returns to investment, labor is a free good and gets no
part of income.

According to Dorfman, this residual is "payment for waiting." I would prefer to say that is payment for the use of "unfinished consumption goods," or "variable capital," or simply "capital." There is payment for waiting only because an increase in the stock of unfinished consumption goods can only be secured by lengthening the period of production. Whatever it is called, this second factor of production, which is created by investing consumption, earns a reward because it has a cost of production and, hence, is scarce. The fact that, by the terms of Dorfman's problem, an additional increment of this second factor cannot be obtained "immediately" is true but essentially irrelevant.

The Period of Production

We can dispose of the view that interest is payment for waiting or abstinence by showing it to be, at worst, the product of terminological confusion and, at best, another name for payment for the use of a productive factor created by investment. The notion of a period of production cannot be excised from capital theory so easily even though the case for excision has been repeatedly and forcefully argued by Frank Knight. By his view:

There is no interval between production and consumption. Any productive act or expenditure always yields its result "instantly," in absolute simultaneity with the production itself, either in the form of service consumed as it is rendered or in the form of a net accretion to assets, i.e., to capital. The complete maintenance, including replacements, of all "equipment" used, is a part of the production of the services currently consumed.[4]

Or again:

[4] *Risk, Uncertainty and Profit* (6th impression; London, 1946), p. xxxviii.

Now, all that is called production in the sense involving a physical product *axiomatically* represents either replacement of capital goods or making a net addition to the total stock. In the one connection the period of production is zero; in the other it is "infinity," ending only with the liquidation of society as a whole.[5]

We shall presently accept that the period of production should be drummed out of capital theory. We cannot, however, do so for the reasons advanced by Knight. It is true that from the accountant's standpoint investment and its rate of return are always computed with respect to the same interval of time; and that this interval may be as long or as short as the accountant cares to make it. Nevertheless, the period of production of a single capital asset is a technical fact. The cost of constructing it may be incurred in one accounting period. Its useful services may accrue in some later accounting period. In capital theory our concern is not with the fictions that accountants employ to reckon rates of return but rather with the net yield of the capital asset during its own particular period of production, i.e., from the moment that the first costs are incurred to construct it to the moment when it gives up its last useful service. Just as there is a period of production for a single item in the capital stock, so also is there an average period of production for all items in the capital stock.

The estimate of the yield on capital that can be obtained from accounting data is only an approximation to the yield on capital as visualized by economists. During the fiscal year, some assets cease to yield any useful service and are scrapped. The initial work begins on other assets

[5] "The Theory of Investment Once More," *Quarterly Journal of Economics*, L (1936), 66–67.

that will give no useful service until some future fiscal year. The most we can say is that when the stock of capital assets is not increasing rapidly—and the ages of capital assets are randomly distributed—these two developments may largely cancel out. On these assumptions, the yield on capital as reckoned from accounting data can be taken as a close approximation to the marginal productivity of investment.

The decisive objection to a place for the period of production in capital theory is not that it is zero or infinity as Knight contends, but rather that, whatever it is, it tells us nothing that we wish to know. Specifically, it does not increase our understanding of how capital assets are valued; nor does it increase our knowledge of the forces that regulate capital accumulation, notably technical change and thrift. The period of production belongs to that large category of constructs that once served a useful purpose in economics but do so no longer. It aided the first stumbling efforts of economists to explain (and justify) the taking of interest. It allowed them to explain why the construction of capital assets is productive. We now know (as W. S. Jevons knew in 1871) that these two objects can be more easily accomplished without the introduction of a period of production into capital theory. Interest, being another name for income, is its own justification. The postulate of continuous technical change is sufficient to establish the possibility of capital accumulation.

In this connection, we might note that the use of the period of production to explain why capital accumulation is possible is the ultimate source of the widely held view that a fall in the rate of interest will lead to a lengthening of the production period, or, in the terminology favored by some writers, to a "deepening of capital." In Robert

Dorfman's version of the Böhm-Bawerk model, this relationship is dictated by the assumptions. When the amount of labor is both fixed and scarce, capital can only be increased by lengthening the production period. Since labor is scarce, capital accumulation is subject to diminishing returns and always occurs in conjunction with a falling rate of interest. It follows that in Dorfman-type models a falling rate of interest is evidence of capital accumulation and, hence, of an increase in the length of the production period.

In the real world, there is, of course, no necessary connection between a change in the rate of interest and a change in the period of production. These two magnitudes may vary inversely but they need not do so. The fact that casual observation shows more time-consuming methods of production to be more productive than more direct methods should not be accepted as evidence against this proposition. As Fisher noted long ago:

It is not true that, of all *possible* productive processes, the longest are the most productive; but it is true that, of all productive processes *actually employed*, the longest are also the most productive. No one will select a long way unless it is at the same time a better way. All the long but unproductive processes are weeded out.[6]

As far as this writer can see, the period of production now serves only one marginally useful purpose in capital theory. It helps to reveal the concept of a marginal productivity of investment (MPI) for the rarefied thing that it is. Even when, following Dorfman, one writes $Y = f(N, p)$ it is exceedingly difficult to reckon MPI; for while an increase in p will "eventually" increase consumable income Y, in

[6] *The Rate of Interest* (New York, 1907), p. 353.

the short run it will cause Y to fall. As we noted in chapter 4, when a period of production is posited, it is necessary to distinguish between the marginal productivity of investment (which gives the rate of interest) and the marginal productivity of capital. Only the marginal productivity of capital $\frac{\Delta Y}{\Delta K}$ can be reckoned directly from the production function. One cannot compute MPI without knowing the quantity of consumption sacrificed; the distribution of this sacrifice over time; the additional income flow that this sacrifice makes possible; and when this flow will begin.

Zero and Negative Rates of Interest

Economists have long been intrigued by the possibility that, in some circumstances, the rate of interest can be zero or even negative. Let us be clear that here our concern is the *real* rate of interest as measured in units of constant purchasing power. As long as money can be stored without cost, the *money* rate of interest cannot be less than zero; and as long as most people exhibit "liquidity preference" the money rate of interest cannot even go as low as zero. Likewise, we are not interested in a world where "less is preferred to more." No doubt a negative real rate of interest would rapidly emerge if most people became convinced that the Day of Judgment were at hand with eternal damnation awaiting all who died rich.

We have observed that when investment entails risk, the grouping of investments in order to reduce risk for the individual investor has a cost, and most investors have an aversion to risk, then a zero or negative rate of interest is possible. This is true whether we are speaking of a pure rate of interest or an average of all interest rates. The meaningful question is: can MPI fall to zero or below?

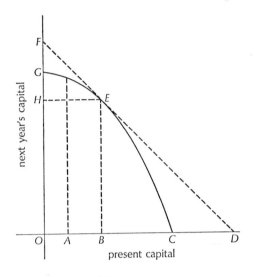

Figure 12.1

Offhand both a zero and a negative MPI would seem to be logical possibilities. Figure 12.1 depicts a Crusonia model with diminishing returns. Once again we assume that the capital stock, in the absence of consumption, grows continuously, and that all consumption for the year takes place now. *OC* gives the present stock of capital. The curve *GC* gives the terms on which present consumption can be exchanged for additional capital next year. Every point on *GC* represents a possible combination of present consumption and future capital. *OD* is equal to *OF*. Therefore, the slope of *GC* at point *E* is equal to unity. The slope of *GC* (−1) gives average MPI for the corresponding quantity of investment. When this quantity is *BC*, MPI is zero. When this quantity is *AC*, MPI is negative. If either *BC* or *AC* is invested, the economy will increase its capital stock during the year.

A moment's reflection will indicate that the geometry of figure 12.1 is highly misleading in two respects. First, it excludes the possibility that income can be stored without cost. If costless storage is possible, the true MPI curve for the Crusonia model in figure 12.1 is *FEC*. Should the economy wish to have the maximum amount of Crusonia available for consumption next year, it will presently consume nothing, harvest and store *OB*, and invest *BC*. At the end of the year, it will possess *OH* units of "live Crusonia and *OB* (or *HF*) units of "dead" Crusonia. When consumption goods can be stored without cost, MPI can fall to zero but no lower.

Figure 12.1 is also misleading in that the possibility of a negative MPI is made to depend upon an unalterable period of production for the "final" product, i.e., consumption. The capital stock grows continuously, yet all consumption takes place once a year on orgy day. Therefore, when investment is carried to the level where MPI is negative, the capital stock reaches its maximum at some moment between orgy days. By the geometry of figure 12.1 the economy can have a capital stock of *OG* next year, if, and only if, it now invests *OC* for the entire year.

If consumption is not limited to one day in the year—if consumption as well as production is continuous—the economy need not invest *OC* in order to attain a capital stock *OG* by the year's end. For consumption itself will serve to retard the fall in MPI during the year. Once MPI has reached zero, the economy gets its best deal on future income by consuming the whole of present income. Actually, to say that consumption and production are continuous is equivalent to saying that capital (or income) can be stored without cost. Our conclusion, to repeat, is that, while MPI can fall to zero, it cannot go below zero unless an unalterable period of production is posited.[7] We could, for example, secure a negative MPI by equating capital with strawberry plants, income with strawberries, and stipulating that strawberries are harvested once a year and cannot be stored.

There remains one other pitfall in this area of capital theory to be noted and avoided. We usually assume that when production and consumption are continuous, there are diminishing returns to investment, and MPI is zero, then the capital stock is at its maximum and hence constant. Note, however, that to obtain this result we must also assume that MPI is solely a function of the size of capital stock.

In chapter 6 we saw that MPI could realistically be viewed as a function of both the size of the capital stock and the level of technology. In chapter 7 we viewed the rate at which obsolete capital assets are retired as a measure of the force of technical progress; for, at any moment in time, the depreciation on obsolete capital is raising the MPI schedule. Given continuous technical progress, income can increase even though the capital stock remains unchanged and capital accumulation is possible with a zero MPI. Indeed, the rate of income growth is maximized by carrying investment to the level where MPI is zero. A positive rate of interest is ordinarily taken to imply a positive MPI. To the extent that this is true, a positive rate of interest is a brake on capital accumulation and not a few writers have drawn the conclusion that a planned economy, by disregarding the market rate of interest in making decisions can increase the rate of capital formation and income growth.

[7] A failure to allow for the possibility that income can be stored without cost or that consumption and investment can be continuous, seems to underlie the most recent demonstration that a negative real rate of interest is possible. Milton Friedman, *Price Theory: A Provisional Text* (Chicago, 1962), pp. 260–62.

By itself this inference is unobjectionable. But some writers go further and use it as a basis for arguing that the level of investment ought to be planned without reference to market rates of interest. This argument merely asserts a personal preference for more rapid income growth, and can be treated as such.

In a market economy, a positive rate of interest is, in a superficial sense, a brake on income growth. Arbitrage keeps the rate of interest on consumption loans equal to MPI; so that, as long as $100 of present consumption exchanges for more than $100 of future income, MPI cannot be zero. In the planned economy there is no reason why MPI and the rate of interest on consumption loans should be equal. Indeed, they cannot be equal if the level of investment is "planned" in any meaningful sense. The efforts of arbitragers to make them equal are economic crimes against the state and must be discouraged. Clearly a firm, which according to the Investment Plan should build a steel mill, cannot be permitted to loan at interest part of its coal allocation to shivering householders merely because the diversion would increase its income and their comfort. (Some economists argue that the planned economy can have any rate of interest that it wishes; but by this term they mean MPI, not the rate of interest on consumption loans.)[8] In fine, the planning of investment presupposes that arbitrage between the consumption and investment uses of income can be suppressed. This can be done—but not easily.

In the *General Theory*, J. M. Keynes argued that in the British economy of the 1930s, a program of state investment subsidies could rapidly have driven the marginal efficiency of capital to zero. While the marginal efficiency of capital

[8] See, for example, Oskar Lange, "On the Economic Theory of Socialism," *Review of Economic Studies*, IV (1936–37), 65–66.

by his definition is not quite the same as MPI as we have defined it, the differences are not significant at this point.[9] That this result could have been secured in a predominantly capitalist economy by subsidies alone is unlikely. Any policy that expands investment at the expense of consumption reduces MPI while simultaneously raising the rate of interest on consumption loans. This gap makes possible an arbitrage profit. Left to their own devices, businessmen will slough off on the maintenance of capital equipment in order to offer additional consumption goods on the loan market. If the "marginal efficiency of capital" is to reach zero, the state must superintend the investment process in order to insure that businessmen do not succumb to the temptations of arbitrage.

The socialist economy that would force MPI below the market rate of interest on consumption loans faces the same problem. To the extent that managers of state enterprises are under strong pressure to meet assigned production targets, the problem is made even more difficult. For the manager's temptation is always to meet his target by diverting resources within the firm from capital maintenance and replacement to the production of items that improve his current production statistics. The real enemy of the Investment Plan is the citizen behaving as a consumer. For it is his perverse preference for present consumption over future income that keeps the rate of interest on consumption loans appreciably above the planned marginal productivity of investment. In a market economy, the ultimate brake on capital formation is not the market rate of interest but the "impatience" rooted in an aversion to risk that insures it.

[9] *The General Theory of Employment, Interest, and Money* (New York, 1936), pp. 375–77. The principal difference is that Keynes' marginal efficiency of capital rests upon subjective estimates of income in a future dimly seen; whereas the MPI of this book is derived from a "known" production function.

If arbitrage can be suppressed, a policy of forced saving can drive MPI to zero. Such a policy would permit the economy to achieve its maximum rate of income growth. It would also reduce economic welfare as the term is understood by most economists.

Recapitulation

Abstinence, the period of production, and zero and negative rates of interest are three topics whose study has generated much bad thinking and even more bad writing in capital theory. Abstinence and the period of production are constructs, never very satisfactory, that are now obsolete. Zero and negative rates of interest are logical possibilities in capital theory. But being neither probable nor desirable, they are not worth the attention that they have received these many years.

CHAPTER 13   Summary

From the materials willed to us by our predecessors from
Thomas Aquinas to Robert Solow, but principally by
Irving Fisher, we have fashioned a complete, if austere,
theory of capital. The theory may briefly be summarized
as follows.

Capital is the only factor of production. The stock of
capital assets is productive in the sense that, in any time
interval, it yields a surplus of services over and above those
needed to maintain and ultimately replace its individual
items. This surplus is income. Every part of income is either
consumed or invested. If consumed, income vanishes, so to
speak, into the cosmos, and is never heard from again. If
invested, income is metamorphosized into additional capital
assets, and income itself is increased by the addition to the
stock of capital assets. In this sense, also, capital is productive: it can be used to create more of itself. An individual
asset in the capital stock is normally created, used for a
time, and scrapped; but a unit of capital viewed as general
productive power goes on forever. "It is fundamental to
the actual phenomenon of capital accumulation that the
principal, once saved, *never is consumed;* if it is consumed
later, there is no net addition to the capital supply of society." [1] The failure of an economy to maintain its capital
stock intact is a logical possibility. At most times and places,
however, capital accumulation is the rule. The population
of capital assets, like the population of human beings, normally has an excess of births over deaths.

[1] Frank Knight, *Risk, Uncertainty, and Profit* (Cambridge, 1921), p. 133.

For a single capital asset, there is clearly a period of production, though it can seldom be measured with exactness. The period begins with the first effort to create an asset that will yield a flow of unique services. It ends when the asset has yielded its last unique services and is consigned to the scrap pile. There is also an *average* period of production for all capital assets. But notwithstanding the bountiful attention they have received in the history of economics, neither of these periods of production is significant in capital theory. (We do not exclude the possibility that they may be relevant to the study of business cycles.) Capital theory can be drastically simplified if we reason "as if" the stock of capital assets increases as income is *not* consumed. The capital stock of the real world may then be regarded as having, in the absence of consumption, a natural growth rate which, together with the economy's taste for investment, determines its actual growth rate. In short, the many periods of production that have played so prominent a role in the development of capital theory are of antiquarian interest only.

When future events are known with perfect certainty, there is but one rate of interest at which capital assets will be borrowed or lent. This rate is equal to the marginal productivity of investment. When there are no diminishing returns to investment, the marginal productivity of investment is the natural growth rate of the capital stock. When there are diminishing returns to investment, it is a function of this natural growth rate.

When future events are not known with perfect certainty, investors normally will exchange investment risks with one another. A capital market emerges in which capital is traded for IOUs that are payable in the future and secured, in whole or in part, by collateral. Since IOUs of the same nominal value can be secured by different amounts of collateral, there will also emerge a set of interest rates. Every interest rate, however, is tied by arbitrage to the marginal productivity of investment. When the future is uncertain, there is no reason why some interest rates in the set should not be zero or even negative. This is true even though the capital stock is increasing at every moment.

The above theory of capital can easily be broadened to accommodate a money commodity that is desired solely as "a medium of exchange and store of value." But the above theory assigns no importance to changes in the supply of, or demand for, money as forces that affect the rate of capital formation. Such changes influence capital formation only to the extent that investors are irrational and the capital market imperfect. The capital theory of this book excludes both possibilities.

In chapter 8 we considered the case where production is carried on with two factors, one fixed in supply, the other capable of being created by investment and destroyed by disinvestment. This examination was undertaken because the assumption that production is carried on with "factors of production" is firmly entrenched in economics; and because the assumption is clearly useful in the study of economic problems where the relevant time span is so short that the cost of changing capital from one specialized form to another is, for all practical purposes, prohibitive. Of necessity, we paid a return visit to venerable issues concerning the nature of a production function. Our principal finding was that "rent" was paid for the use of the fixed factor, and that rent is a surplus which remains after the variable factor is compensated at a rate equal to the marginal productivity of investment. Chapter 9 examined the case where production is carried on with two factors of production, neither of which was fixed in supply. The problem of working technical progress into the production function was here briefly considered.

In this book, we have had occasion to examine a number of issues that have long plagued economists. At the heart of everybody's capital theory is the assumption that income will be greater in the future if some part of present income is invested. That investment in capital assets is productive economists do not doubt. But they differ in their explanations as to why this is so. This lack of consensus is understandable given the "fact" that capital accumulation is bound up with the creation and application of new knowledge, whereas economists not only do not know much about how new knowledge is created and applied but have only recently begun to devise ways of thinking about the problem.

To date, economists have relied heavily on the aid of analogies to make the concept of capital productivity intelligible to themselves and others. Hence, the popularity in capital theory of one commodity models—aging wine, growing trees, multiplying rabbits, etc. The efforts of some writers to relate capital productivity to the length of the period of production or the mysterious process by which the application of human labor to inanimate materials yields surplus value have merely puzzled and confused generations of readers.

In this book we have cheerfully accepted the advisability of proceeding by analogy. Capital has been likened to the Crusonia plant, a species of all-purpose vegetation that, in the absence of consumption of Crusonia, grows. Two expository merits are claimed for this device. It largely eliminates the "period of production" and so makes possible a precise delineation of the marginal productivity of investment—the fundamental concept in capital theory. It is the simplest analogue yet discovered for representing capital productivity and so minimizes the opportunities for error. (It is probably the simplest analogue that ever will be discovered.)

Our analysis has touched upon the venerable issue of returns to investment. We saw that most capital assets are specialized to a few uses in the short run; that an effort to accelerate the rate of capital formation would require the diversion of specialized assets to new and unanticipated uses; and that the greater this diversion, the greater the cost in consumption sacrificed. In the short run, the existence of diminishing returns to investment is insured by the very fact of specialization. Nevertheless, at any given moment, some fully depreciated and obsolete assets are being replaced by superior men or machines. The marginal productivity of investment is perforce a function of these opposing forces. Depending upon which is the stronger, and also on the taste for investment, the return to investment, in any accounting period, may rise or fall.

We have seen that when investment is associated with risk, a market for IOUs will emerge in which these risks are exchanged; that in such a market both the pure and the average rate of interest will normally be below the marginal productivity of investment; and that either or both of these interest rates may be zero or negative. We related the minimum rate of interest to the cost of organizing insurance programs for investors and the maximum rate of interest to the cost of organizing lotteries for gamblers. Chapter 11 examined the demand for money as a determinant of interest rates and suggested that people hold money in excess of their transactions needs for the same reason that they hold IOUs—that is, to escape or assume the risks of real investment. Chapter 12 considered three venerable issues in capital theory that are now mainly of antiquarian interest—abstinence, the period of production, and zero and negative rates of interest.

A Final Reflection

Our capital theory has been expounded without reference to any particular "rules of the game," capitalist or socialist, or to any particular state of the industrial arts. The result is a theory of value of a type whose usefulness has not infrequently been questioned, most recently by Mrs. Robinson. "Economic analysis, serving for two centuries to win an understanding of the Nature and Causes of the Wealth of Nations, has been fobbed off with another bride—a Theory of Value." [2] In defense of the efforts required to read and write this book, it may be urged that a theory of value, notwithstanding its obvious limitations, is indispensable equipment for anyone who undertakes to explore the mysteries of economic progress.

There *is* a stock of capital assets, though opinions may differ on the wisdom of including or excluding particular items. Income *can* be increased by adding to this stock. This stock *can* be increased by investing income. The value of an individual capital asset is always some approximation to the sum of its future payments as discounted by investors, speculators, or the Central Planning Commission. The rate used to discount the future payments of the single asset is determined by the prospective yields on alternative investments. Admittedly, a clear view of the process by which capital assets are valued, in so far as investors, speculators, and the Central Planning Commission believe that they can foresee the future, is no substitute for that far nobler and unattainable thing—a complete theory of economic prog-

[2] *The Accumulation of Capital* (London, 1956), p. v.

ress. It does, however, allow one to undertake more ambitious investigations without the ever-present danger of mistaking a change in the value of capital assets for a change in real capital stock, erroneously equating the marginal productivity of investment with some particular rate of interest in the real world, misunderstanding the role of interest rates in capital formation, or being distracted by such irrelevancies as the period of production. A theory of capital, for which these merits can fairly be claimed, even if it is *mere* value theory, is no mean achievement.

APPENDIXES

APPENDIX A   Ramsey, Bliss, and Fisher

Many years ago the Cambridge mathematician F. P. Ramsey offered a treatment of investment that is, in some respects, more general than the Fisher-type treatment of this book which relies upon indifference curves.[1] In Ramsey's treatment, the time span to which the investment decision relates extends to infinity; and using Ramsey's method it is possible to compute the optimal rate of investment at every moment in time. Since Ramsey's treatment of investment was set forth in a rather abstract article which uses an awkward notation, shows signs of hasty composition, and employs a mathematical technique (the calculus of variations) not universally included in the education of economists, there may be merit in going over the ground once more.[2] One other reason for undertaking the review can be cited. Ramsey is the source of the arresting but patently suspect proposition that, when the utility of future consumption is not subjectively discounted, "the amount we should save out of a given income is entirely independent of the present rate of interest, unless this rate is actually zero."[3] In Ramsey's model the rate of interest is another name for the marginal productivity of investment.

Ramsey's model is of the Crusonia type familiar to us. The addition to income resulting from investment begins to flow immediately; all units in the capital stock are identical. Let

K = capital

Y = income

---

[1] "A Mathematical Theory of Saving," *Economic Journal*, XXXVIII (1928), 543–59.

[2] Not that Ramsey's treatment of investment has gone unnoted. See P. A. Samuelson and R. M. Solow, "A Complete Capital Model Involving Heterogeneous Capital Goods," *Quarterly Journal of Economics*, LXX (1956), 537–39.

[3] "A Mathematical Theory of Saving," p. 548.

C = consumption

r = marginal productivity of investment (rate of interest)

$Y - C = \dfrac{dK}{dt}$ = saving

$U = f(C)$ = total utility of consumption

$M = f'(C)$ = marginal utility of consumption given that $M = 0$ when $C = C^*$

When $M = 0$, the economy may be said to have achieved "ultimate bliss," the ecstatic state which we mundanely designate B_1. However, it may be neither possible nor desirable to reach ultimate bliss. The rate of interest may fall to zero before $M = 0$. In this event, the economy achieves "attainable bliss," designated B_2, when the rate of interest is zero. The economy may subjectively discount the utility of future consumption. If so, "modified bliss," designated B_3, is achieved when the rate of interest is equal to the subjective discount rate. Thus $B_1 > B_2 > B_3$.

The investment problem of the economy is to reach the relevant bliss level as defined by technology, resources, and taste in the least painful way. Some pain is inevitable (assuming that bliss has not yet been achieved) since bliss can be more closely approached only by foregoing consumption in order to increase the capital stock.

A vast number of "intertemporal" saving patterns will serve to move the economy toward the relevant bliss level. The problem is to find the saving pattern that will minimize welfare loss ("pain") L which must be incurred in the journey. Suppose that it is technically possible to reach ultimate bliss, B_1, and that the utility of future consumption is not subjectively discounted. The utility derived from the consumption of next year is as highly valued as that derived from consumption now. On these assumptions the investment problem of Ramsey is simply to minimize:

$$L = \int_0^\infty (B_1 - U)\, dt \qquad (1)$$

In equation (1) we can change the independent variable from t to K by multiplying each side by $dK/dt \div dK/dt$. We can substitute a and b_1 as the limits of integration where a is the size of the capital stock now and b_1 is the size of the capital needed for ultimate bliss. Then

$$L = \int_a^{b_1} \frac{(B_1 - U)}{\dfrac{dK}{dt}} \, dK \tag{1a}$$

or

$$L = \int_a^{b_1} \frac{(B_1 - U)}{(Y - C)} \, dK \tag{1b}$$

It is reasonable to assume that there exists some minimum value for L since, at any given income level, some saving patterns are preferred to others. In equation (1b), if such a minimum value for the integral exists, it can be found by minimizing the integrand for each increment of capital independently. Since we can fix consumption C for each level of capital K, we minimize by differentiating the integrand with respect to C (K being constant) and equating the result to zero. (Recall that $U = f(C)$ and $M = f'(C)$.) Performing this operation we get

$$\frac{B_1 - U_2}{(Y - C)^2} - \frac{M}{Y - C} = 0 \tag{2}$$

or

$$Y - C = \frac{dK}{dt} = \frac{B_1 - U}{M} \tag{2a}$$

Note that in equation (2a) dK/dt depends only on the utility function, its upper bound B_1, and its derivative M. In equation (2a) dK/dt does not depend on the rate of interest. It was this circumstance that seems to have led Ramsey to the conclusion that the amount which the economy should save out of a given income is independent of the present rate of interest, unless this rate be zero. This result, if valid, would have had rather serious implications for all previous work in capital theory. However, other parts of Ramsey's analysis can be used to show that the values of the variables M and U in equation (2a) are not independent of the rate of interest.

Let us continue with the case where future utilities and present utilities are equally valued. At any moment, the economy maximizes welfare by equating the utility of an increment of consumption now to the utility of an increment of consumption postponed for a few seconds. When the rate of interest is r, an increment of consumption ΔC will, if postponed these few seconds until time t, grow to $\Delta C(1 + r)^t$. Let M denote the marginal utility of current income consumed now and M_t the marginal utility of current income consumed the few seconds later at time t. Then welfare is maximized when

$$M = M_t(1 + r)^t \tag{3}$$

Now
$$\frac{dM}{dt} = -M_t(1 + r)^t \log_e (1 + r) \tag{4}$$

When $t \to 0$, equation (4) becomes

$$\frac{dM}{dt} = -M \log_e (1 + r) \tag{5}$$

or
$$M = \frac{-\dfrac{dM}{dt}}{\log_e (1 + r)} \tag{5a}$$

In equation (5)[4] the instantaneous rate of interest is $\log_e (1 + r)$. Therefore, at any moment, welfare is maximized when "the marginal utility of consumption falls at a proportionate rate given by the rate of interest."[5] Since the variable M appears in both equation (5a) and equation (2a), the latter can be written as

$$Y - C = -\frac{(B_1 - U) \log_e (1 + r)}{\dfrac{dM}{dt}} \tag{2b}$$

Thus we return to Irving Fisher's world where the rate of interest (defined as the marginal productivity of investment) is a determinant of saving. Ramsey's apparent conclusion to the

---

[4] In equation (5) the right-hand side is given a negative sign because, as long as some part of income is saved, consumption is growing and dM/dt is negative.

[5] "A Mathematical Theory of Saving," p. 546.

contrary is seen to be misleading. Strictly speaking, of course, it is not profitable to inquire how the rate of interest affects the willingness of the economy to save out of a "given" income. For when the capital stock is given, income is perforce specified whenever the rate of interest is specified. Should the rate of interest be raised by technical progress, the capital stock remaining unchanged, income increases *pari passu* and one gets a new "given" income.

If the goal is attainable bliss, rather than ultimate bliss (because the rate of interest falls to zero before ultimate bliss is reached), we substitute B_2 for B_1 in equation (1), write the upper limit of integration as b_2, and proceed as before. If all future utilities are subjectively discounted by the constant factor p, the investment goal becomes the achievement of modified bliss B_3 with the least pain, the upper limit of integration becomes b_3 and the "effective" rate of discount of utilities becomes $(r - p)$. The optimum amount of saving out of income is now given by

$$Y - C = -\frac{(B_3 - U) \log_e (1 + r - p)}{\dfrac{dM}{dt}} \qquad (6)$$

Equation (6) is suggested by Ramsey's article but is not explicit in it. Ramsey does not give a clear lead at this point since, in order to simplify his equations containing the subjective discount factor p, he makes r and p positive constants independent of K. When $r > p$, the capital stock grows until $M = 0$. When $r < p$, the capital stock shrinks until wholly consumed. When for all values of K we have $r > p > 0$, then the economy's investment goal is really ultimate bliss B_1. The introduction of the subjective discount factor p reduces the fraction of income saved and so lengthens the time required to reach B_1. It does not change the bliss level aimed at. Modified bliss B_3 becomes the investment goal only when, for some value of K ($K = b_3$), $r = p$ and $M > 0$.

Using Ramsey's method, we confirm that there are three situations in which a constant stock of capital is either reached or asymptotically approached as a limit: 1) When consumers are sated with utilities ($B_1 = U$); 2) When it is no longer possible to increase income by saving $(r = p = 0)$; 3) When the marginal rate of preference for present over future utilities is equal to the rate of interest $(p = r)$.

These three equilibria we have met in a different guise in chapter 6.

The mathematical problems of discovering the optimal path of capital formation over time are, of course, more numerous and difficult than this brief discussion of Ramsey's work may have suggested. Most notably, once we drop the assumption that production is carried on with Crusonia or some malleable surrogate capital, we collide with the much discussed turnpike problem.[6] As Samuelson and others have shown, when capital goods are specialized, the investment pattern which is optimal between two given points in time may not—and probably will not—be optimal at any single moment.[7]

[6] Notably in the symposium on "Prices and the Turnpike," *Review of Economic Studies*, XXVIII, No. 2 (1961), 77–104.

[7] R. Dorfman, R. M. Solow, and P. A. Samuelson, *Linear Programming and Economic Analysis* (New York, 1958), pp. 309–16.

APPENDIX B   Technical Progress
"Embodied" in New Machines

While the idea that the growth of knowledge has little or no economic pay-off until incorporated in new capital assets is not new, its systematic elaboration dates from a pioneer article by Leif Johansen[1] that appeared in 1959. Since then the number of growth models which embody technical progress, some of them quite elaborate, has increased rapidly. However, the first principles of how to embody technical progress in a growth model can be demonstrated with the aid of the simplest version of R. M Solow's well-known model.[2] We limit our attention to it.

Assume that every capital asset ("machine") represents the latest in technology at the time of its construction, has its technical efficiency fixed once and for all at birth, and remains in use forever. Finally assume that, within wide limits, any capital asset can be employed with any quantity of labor.

Let $G(t)$ denote the level of technology at time t. Let $G(t)$ increase neutrally and exponentially at the rate λ. Now $K_v(t)$ can be the quantity of capital of vintage v (i.e., produced at time v) where $t \geq v$. Likewise $N_v(t)$ can be the quantity of labor used with $K_v(t)$. Let the output $Y_v(t)$ obtained by using $K_v(t)$ with $N_v(t)$ be given by

$$Y_v(t) = G_0 e^{\lambda v} K_v(t)^{1-b} N_v(t)^b \qquad (1)$$

Total output at time t is found by summing up the outputs of machines of all different vintages.

[1] "Substitution versus Fixed Production Coefficients in the Theory of Economic Growth: A Synthesis," *Econometrica*, XXVII (1959), 157–76.
[2] "Investment and Technical Progress," in *Mathematical Methods in the Social Sciences*, K. J. Arrow, ed. (Stanford, 1960), pp. 89–104.

$$Y(t) = \int_{-\infty}^{t} Y_v(t) \, dv \tag{2}$$

Total stock of capital at time t is, of course,

$$K(t) = \int_{-\infty}^{t} K_v(t) \, dv \tag{3}$$

Since factor proportions are variable, labor will be allocated so that its marginal product is the same on all machines. Thus the marginal product of labor is not affected by the age of the machine on which it is employed. If $m(t)$ denotes the marginal product of labor

$$m(t) = \frac{\partial Y_v(t)}{\partial N_v(t)} = bG_0e^{\lambda v}K_v(t)^{1-b}N_v(t)^{b-1} \tag{4}$$

Then
$$N_v(t) = (bG_0)^{\frac{1}{1-b}}m(t)^{\frac{1}{b-1}}e^{\frac{\lambda v}{1-b}}K_v(t) \tag{4a}$$

or
$$N_v(t) = h(t)e^{\frac{\lambda v}{1-b}}K_v(t) \tag{4b}$$

and
$$N(t) = \int_{-\infty}^{t} N_v(t) \, dv \tag{5}$$

or
$$N(t) = h(t) \int_{-\infty}^{t} e^{\frac{\lambda v}{1-b}}K_v(t) \, dv \tag{5a}$$

Substituting (4b) in (1) and simplifying, we have

$$Y_v(t) = G_0e^{\frac{\lambda v}{1-b}} h(t)^b K_v(t) \tag{6}$$

Together (5a) and (6) yield

$$Y(t) = G_0J(t)^{1-b} N(t)^b \tag{7}$$

where
$$J(t) = \int_{-\infty}^{t} e^{\frac{\lambda v}{1-b}}K_v(t) \, dv$$

The J variable is sometimes termed "effective capital" to distinguish it from physical capital K. But this designation is rather confusing since J is not the value of the capital stock K in terms of current income Y. In fact, J is merely an index of the productive capacity of machinery obtained by weighting each unit of capital according to its date of birth. The latest bit of capital is, of course, weighted with the biggest λv.

However, at time t, the value of the capital stock in terms of current income—this value is capital's share of income divided by the marginal productivity of investment—is a function of J. Call this capitalized factor share $A(t)$. Since the capitalization process insures that, when factor supplies are expressed as their income equivalents, payments to the factors exhaust the product,

$$Y(t) = G_0 e^{\lambda t} A(t)^{1-b} N(t)^b \qquad (8)$$

and from (7) and (8)

$$A(t) = \frac{J(t)}{e^{\frac{\lambda t}{1-b}}}$$

For the record we note that the marginal productivity of investment (in new machines) at time t is given by the value for r which satisfies

$$rA(t) = (1 - b) Y(t) \qquad (10)$$

Thus in terms of the variables in the original production function given by equation (1)

$$r = \frac{(1 - b) Y(t) e^{\frac{\lambda t}{1-b}}}{\displaystyle\int_{-\infty}^{t} e^{\frac{\lambda v}{1-b}} K_v(t) \, dv} \qquad (10a)[3]$$

The above model that embodies technical progress only in new machines can easily be made more complicated. For example, in the interest of greater realism we could posit that some machines are destroyed by use or accident, that once built every machine has a fixed labor requirement for all of its life, or that technical progress is embodied in both old and new machines. However, any model of economic activity that is

---

[3] For a more elaborate discussion of investment returns in models where income grows exponentially see James Tobin, "Economic Growth as an Object of Government Policy," *American Economic Review*, LIV, No. 3 (1964), 1–20.

based on a distinction between capital and labor is already so far from reality that not much realism is regained by tinkering with its other assumptions. Therefore, my own preference is for resolving all doubts in favor of simple growth models.

APPENDIX C   Interest Rates, Risk,
and Equilibrium in Capital Markets

In a world of risk, the concept of "equilibrium" in the capital
market is exceedingly difficult to formulate with precision. Three
obstacles especially impede the effort.

First, the marginal productivity of investment (MPI) viewed
as a random variable, as in chapter 10, may be affected by an
increase in the size of the capital stock. One or both of two things
may happen. The mathematical value of MPI may change.
The dispersion of possible investment outcomes about the mean
may change. When an increase in the capital stock produces
either of these results, there can be no equilibrium set of interest
rates on IOUs as long as the capital stock continues to increase.
For the interest rates in the set must themselves be continuously
changing.

Second, even though the mathematical value of MPI is not
altered by a change in the capital stock, the taste for risk may
be affected, so that the composition or mix of the IOUs (classified according to risk) in the capital market may change. For
example, as the capital stock grows, the demand for high-risk
IOUs may rise more rapidly than the demand for safe IOUs.

We can circumvent these two obstacles by stipulating that
both MPI viewed as a random variable and the taste for risk
are independent of the size of the capital stock. Nevertheless, a
third obstacle to the determination of equilibrium will remain.
The supply of, and demand for, any one type of IOU depends
upon the terms on which other types of IOUs can be bought
and sold; and the number of these alternatives depends, in part,
upon the taste for risk. We deal with this last obstacle in the
following way.

Let $M = (m_1, m_2, \ldots, m_n)$ denote the investment function with m_1 being the least favorable outcome that is possible and m_n being the most favorable

$T = (t_1, t_2, \ldots, t_z)$ denote the taste for risk with z signifying the number of individual investors

$L = (l_1, l_2, \ldots, l_y)$ denote the set of all possible loans secured by different percentages of collateral with l_1 being a fully secured loan and l_y a wholly unsecured loan

$R = (r_1, r_2, \ldots, r_y)$ denote the set of interest rates corresponding to the loans $l_1, l_2, \ldots, l_y$

$E(M) =$ the mathematical value of M

$g =$ the cost of grouping individual investments to insure a gross return equal to $E(M)$, g being a percent of the sum invested

$h =$ the cost of organizing a lottery, h being a percent of the sum wagered

$g < E(M) - m_1$

$h < m_n - E(M)$

The last two conditions insure that the costs of organizing investment insurance programs and lotteries are not "prohibitive" and hence irrelevant to the problem of equilibrium in the capital market.

Consider now the taste for risk of the ith investor as indicated by his willingness to buy and sell different types of IOUs. For every type of IOU he faces three mutually exclusive alternatives; he may buy, sell, or remain out of the market. Given y different types of IOUs, $l_1, l_2, \ldots, l_y$, we can write the following supply-demand functions:

$$l_{1i} = f_{1i}(r_1, r_2, \ldots, r_y)$$
$$l_{2i} = f_{2i}(r_1, r_2, \ldots, r_y)$$
$$l_{yi} = f_{yi}(r_1, r_0 \quad \cdots)$$

(1)

When $l_{1i} > 0$, the ith investor buys IOUs of type l_1 and so lends capital. When $l_{1i} < 0$, the ith investor sells IOUs of type l_1 and so borrows capital. When $l_{1i} = 0$, the ith investor is "out of the market" for IOUs of type l_1.

Should the ith investor be offered less than y alternatives in the capital market, say s alternatives, his set of supply-demand functions becomes

$$l_{1i} = \phi_{1i}(r_1, r_2, \ldots, r_s)$$
$$l_{2i} = \phi_{2i}(r_1, r_2, \ldots, r_s)$$
$$\cdots\cdots\cdots\cdots\cdots$$
$$l_{si} = \phi_{si}(r_1, r_2, \ldots, r_s) \tag{2}$$

For the capital market to be in equilibrium, for every different type of IOU the quantity supplied must equal the quantity demanded. If there are z investors and y different types of IOU are offered, the equilibrium conditions are

$$\sum_1^z l_1 = 0$$
$$\sum_1^z l_2 = 0 \tag{3}$$
$$\cdots\cdots$$
$$\sum_1^z l_y = 0$$

However, it may not be possible to find a set of interest rates, $R = (r_1, r_2, \ldots, r_y)$ that allows the conditions of (3) to be satisfied. For the range of interest rates has both an upper and a lower bound. The possibility of organizing an insurance program for investors insures that for every r,

$$r \geq E(M) - g \tag{4}$$

And the possibility of organizing lotteries insures that for every r,

$$r \leq E(M) + h \tag{5}$$

Should no equilibrium be possible when y different types of IOUs are offered on the capital market, some type or types of IOUs will disappear. This contraction of choice will serve to increase both the supply of, and demand for, the types of IOUs that remain on the market. The process of contraction will continue until there exists a set of interest rates that equates the quantity supplied and quantity demanded for every type of IOU traded. Conceivably, the process of contraction could continue until the capital market disappeared entirely. This unlikely event could come to pass, however, only if all investors had identical tastes for risk and identical opportunities to invest, so that the *raison d'être* at a capital market would no longer exist.

Subject Index

Abstinence, 33, 96, 197

Adding-up problem: capitalization and, 123; described, 115–16

Bliss: how achieved, 88–89, 221–22; varieties of, 222

Capital: as abstract productive power, 28–29; as discounted income, 30–31, 171; as one factor of production, 114; as only factor of production, 24–25; as stock of specialized assets, 28–29; as unfinished consumption goods, 200; defined, 23–24; measured, 168–71

Capital assets, replacement of, 50, 99–107

Capital market: arbitrage in, 56, 168, 199; disappearance of, 233–34; equilibrium in, 231–34; insurance and, 158–59; lotteries and, 159–60; purpose of, 156

Capital productivity: "brute fact" of, 9; explanations of, 36–48; importance of, 33; technical progress and, 7, 44–45

Capital structure, 47

Capital theory: analogies in, 8–9, 48–49; Austrian, 97; circular reasoning in, 34, 48; described, 1; Lerner on, 106–11; methodology of, 7; terminology of, 4–5

Central banking, philosophy of, 5

Consumer durables, 21–22

Consumption: definitions of, 21, 24; how maximized, 136–37

Consumption function, Friedman on, 24

Contractual interest, 160

Crusonia model: introduced, 80; with risk, 152–53

Das Kapital, 47

Demand for money, see Money

Depreciation: how reckoned, 22; specialization and, 28, 105; ubiquity of, 20

Diminishing returns to investment: controversy over, 94; in Austrian capital theory, 97; in long run, 89–90; in short run, 83–84; with a fixed factor, 97

Discount rate, choice of, 170

Distribution, marginal productivity theory of: ambiguities in, 123; origins of, 116; resistance to, 129

Economic growth: model of, 130–38; sources of, 143–47

Factor shares, distribution of: according to Allais, 119; according to Marshall, 129; according to Wicksell, 116

Gambling, see Lotteries

Growth, see Economic growth

Human capital, 27, 46

Impatience, 70, 210

Income, definitions of, 18–24

Indifference curves: an objection to, 76–77; introduced, 72–76

Innovation, see Technical progress

Insurance, see Investment insurance

Interest, see Rate of interest

Interest theory, see Capital theory; monetary theory of interest

Investment: definitions of, 20–24; economic growth and, 131–36; education as, 27; effect on interest rate, 192–93; slave-breeding as, 27

Investment insurance, 158–59

IOUs, see Capital market

Labor: as capital, 24; as "ultimate" factor of production, 199; problems of measuring, 145–46

Labor theory of value, 40, 41

Land: as capital, 24; as fixed factor of production, 117
Liquidity preference, 174
Lotteries: as alternative to investment, 71, 159–60; cost of, 164
Lucrum cessans, 36
Marginal efficiency of capital, 209–10
Marginal efficiency of investment, 108
Marginal productivity of capital, 60–61, 108–9
Marginal productivity of investment: as a random variable, 152; capital accumulation and, 106–7; defined, 51–52; similar concepts, 51; technology and, 91
Marginal rate of return over cost, 14
Medieval interest theory, 36
Monetary theory of interest: assumptions of, 176; central banking and, 196; omission in, 189; versus real capital theory, 175, 194
Money: in Colonial America, 176; speculative demand for, 185–92; transaction demand for, 180–85; utility of, 175–77
Money illusion: described, 177; doubtful significance of, 178–79
Money market, *see* Capital market
National income accounting, described, 18–22
Negative interest, 158, 205–6
Perfect competition, defined, 128–29
Period of production: Böhm-Bawerk on, 40–41; Fisher on, 204; Knight on, 201–2
Planned economy, investment and, 209–11
Price level, interest rate and, 182–85
Prices, rigidity of, 179
Production function: in static state, 98; "surrogate," 79; technical change and, 138–43
Production techniques, spectrum of, 43
Profit: as payment for waiting, 198; Weston's theory of, 170
Pure interest, 151

Rate of interest: connotations of, 150–51; in a planned economy, 209–11; insurance and, 158–59; lotteries and, 159–62; price level and, 182–85; storage costs and, 91, 207
Rent, capitalization of, 123
Returns to scale: discussed, 117–26; monopoly and, 122–23
"Ricardo effect," discussed, 126–29
Risk: capital formation and, 167–68; capital market and, 154; investor attitudes toward, 156; law of large numbers and, 169; uncertainty and, 170
Saving, *see* Investment
Say's law, 105
Slave-breeding, as investment, 27
Static state, concept of, 45, 97–100
"Surrogate capital," 79, 226
Taste for investment: described, 69; income changes and, 86–87; risk and, 70–71; time-preference and, 70
Taste for risk: capital formation and, 167–68; effect on interest rate, 92
Technical progress: economic growth and, 143–47; "embodied," 227–30; how measured, 140–41; investment and, 107–8; "organizational," 146–47; production function and, 138–39; profit and, 7; value of capital and, 30
Technology, as "inexhaustible capital," 142
Thrift, *see* Taste for investment
Time-preference: importance to Fisher, 15; objections to, 70–71
Turnpike problem, 226
Uncertainty, distinguished from risk, 170
Usury, Medieval attitudes to, 36
Utility, how maximized, 81–89, 221–26
Wages, rigidity of, 179
Waiting, 33, 197, 201
Welfare, *see* Utility
Zero interest, 158, 205–6, 225

Author Index